To faith, family, and friends; and to my late husband, Kelland K. Jeffords, who taught me that these are the most important things in life.

LIFE

Your life is only but a vapor
That will soon vanish away
You do not have the promise of tomorrow
Not even the promise of today.

Why spend your life here in pleasure
Seeking the world and its fame
For when you meet the white throne judgment
You will stand before God in shame.

Your life's record is being kept in Heaven
To be presented to you that day,
If Jesus says He never knew you
There is nothing you can say.

So search God's Holy Scriptures
You can surely find the way.
And the Son of Man will redeem you
That great and noble day.

by

Charles Raymond Jeffords

ISBN-10: 1-59684-270-9
ISBN-13: 978-1-59684-270-0

Printed by Derek Press, Cleveland, Tennessee

I have thought of writing a book on the life of my late husband, Kelland K. Jeffords, for several years. Why? I have always felt his life ended too soon. He had so much more to give. At the time of his death, April 22, 1987, there was more love to be shown. He didn't let sickness interfere with his ministerial duties. He was happiest when he was serving his beloved church, his family, and his many friends. I couldn't understand then and I still do not apprehend now why he had to die at the young age of fifty-eight years.

To have had a life that was filled with so many *wonderful* people and happenings is not a bad thing. You will read in this book how some of his *dearest* friend's lives were touched by his ministry. The *inspiration* received from this man, who motivated them to strive for greater things.

His devotion to family is noteworthy. Our children, Dianne, Keith, and Danita, are achievers and are reaching their godly potential because of his encouragement and belief in them. He challenged them to be their best in whatever vocation they would choose.

Kelland always had time for our children. That was important to him. They were three very talented children that would make any parent proud. When I was working, he sacrificed his time to see they got to their piano, trumpet, or voice lessons. Their training was important to him. It was up to us, the parents, to see our children's talent fully developed. It took time and money. It never was a question for him. He faithfully did his part as a father.

Over the years, our home was always open to friends of our children. Dozens of youth spent their summers with us. Others lived in our home until they could find work, even if it took months. He enjoyed talking and sharing with them events of his own personal life. Those young people would leave better off than when they came.

He had a successful ministry. In whatever capacity he served, the church benefited. The growth of the church during his pastorate set new records in attendance, finance, and membership. He pointed their thinking in a new direction. They would never have a feeling of "*status quo*" again. He taught them to reach for goals and heights that were achievable. Keep reaching for the next level.

This, I felt, needed to be passed on to other ministers that would follow after him. His earthly ministry had ended. But, somehow I knew his *enthusiastic spirit* needed to be shared with generations to come.

The first step in this direction was to endow a scholarship at Lee University, his Alma Mater. Family and friends gave generously to make it possible. As his family, we are happy to make it possible for Georgia students to pursue their educational goals at a Christ-centered college.

Second, this book will help students know about the man for whom the scholarship is named: 1) His love for young people. 2) His enthusiasm for the ministry. 3) His loving care for humanity. 4) His challenge to achieve the unachievable. 5) His devotion to family. 6) His commitment to the church. 7) His godly wisdom used in all things.

If these noble characteristics can be passed on to generations who follow him, surely it will be worth the effort.

Also, I mention in this book a lot of humorous events. Kelland enjoyed life to the fullest. He could find *humor* anywhere and in anything. His *optimism* was clearly evident when you were around him, if only for a short time. He was a lovable and likeable person!

To those who have taken time to write memories about this man who was 'bigger than life", I am forever grateful. I have left out so many friends and happenings, and I hope you will forgive me. There is not enough space and time to tell all the good things about one so loved. You know who you are, and I want you to know how much I love and appreciate you!

I want to give "special thanks" to Jim Grimes, Annette Cool and Bob Florance who assisted me in putting the book together.

Nelia Jeffords-McDaniel

April 26, 1987. A new life began for my family. For thirty-seven extraordinary years, my life had revolved around Kelland Jeffords life and his ministry. It was a fun-filled and full-filled life with him. The phone always ringing and people coming by for a visit gave us a sense of belonging. We were responsible to the Rainbow Drive Church of God congregation, and they were answerable to us. It was a comfortable feeling.

The days following Kelland's death on April 22, 1987 didn't leave any time for loneliness. Our house on Hapsburg Court in Decatur was filled with people coming and going. People bringing food; phone calls from family and friends; others paying their condolences. And, there were details for the funeral to take care of. For the next four days, it was a busy time for me. It seemed there were a thousand things to think about.

After the burial in Jesup, Georgia, which was two hundred and fifty miles from Decatur, we returned home. The house was so empty. But, it was home. Just six months before, we had bought the parsonage; the first house we ever owned. Back then, many preachers' wives had to start thinking of a place to live after the death of their spouse. Thank God this was not the case for me. At least I didn't have to move.

Keith was living at home while enrolled as a third year student at Emory University School of Dentistry. I was thankful that I would not be totally alone. Even though he would be in and out, there was this feeling of alienation. Suddenly, I felt detached from the church. I was so alone. The tears flowed freely day and night. It was as if a part of me was missing. I had my career with Bristol-Myers Squibb that would keep my time occupied and I was thankful. All my life had been centered around church. I couldn't believe that part of my life was over, not at fifty-three years of age. I guess what I'm trying to say is, "I needed to be needed".

None of us are indispensable. The Rainbow Church of God would continue to function as a church with or without the Jeffords family. The work of God must go on. That is a given. But, is it wrong to expect this to evolve with time? In 1987, I would liked for it to have been a gradual process. But, it wasn't. It happened rather quickly. The church had just lost their pastor. Not only did I loose my pastor, but I lost my husband, my companion, my best friend, my confidant, and my prayer partner.

We had never failed or neglected our responsibility as pastor and wife. Kelland's sickness did not interfere when it came to administering his duties to the church. Many times he didn't feel like it, but sick or well, he was on the job. The people never knew of his sacrifice because he didn't complain. He was faithful to visit the sick at home or in the hospital. He was always available when called on. He was just a phone call away.

I was naïve enough to think the church would still need me to play the piano for them. I only missed one Sunday following his burial on Friday and the next Sunday I was back in church. When I walked in church, there was a young lady sitting at the piano. I had been replaced. Was the Lord telling me that it was time to move on?

I'm sure those weeks that Kelland was in the hospital fighting for his life, the church started thinking about a replacement. It was evident without a divine miracle from God he would not live. The church was loosing their shepherd. It was a comfort to know they had the assistant pastor in this time of loss to stand with them.

However, it was difficult for me when I got a phone call from one of the men of the church the next week asking when I could clear out Kelland's office. The night that he called, I was crying, as I did so often, and told him I would have it cleaned out within two or three days. Dianne and Danita went with me. We packed up and removed all of Kelland's books, personal effects, pictures, etc. from the church we had served for almost seven years. I knew I would have to vacate his office, but not that soon. In between times of crying our heart out, we got through with the task. It seemed so final. His office was so empty. We said good-by in our silence as we left the Rainbow Drive Church of God.

Starting over.

In retrospect, it was the best thing for me. Keith, Danita, and I transferred our membership to Mt. Paran Church of God. Dr. Walker and the Mt. Paran congregation welcomed us with open arms. It was a healing time for me to sit under the ministry of our long time friend, Dr. Paul L. Walker. His sermons week after week were a healing balm and ministered to me personally. Dr. Walker and Carmelita were faithful shepherds and knew how to care for their sheep. Mt. Paran Church of God is a true New Testament church. Thank you Paul and Carmelita for your love and support when I needed it most.

What a difference in my life that took place in April 1987. Starting over again was rough. I had my career with Bristol-Myers Squibb, so I plunged myself into my work winning award after award, promotion after promotion. There were no answers to the *why's* and *where to now* question. In my depth of desperation, the Lord let me know the chapters of Kelland and Nelia's life had been written. It was finished. But, my life was not over and there is more yet to be written. What an awesome God we serve...What a loving Saviour...What a wonderful life he has given us!

Nelia Flowers-Jeffords

CONTENTS

Chapter 1

Early Childhood

Kelland Keith Jeffords was born October 26, 1928 in Waresboro, Georgia, the second son of *Clyde and Isabel Jeffords*. Born at home, his birth was recorded as "Jeffords boy", and was given his full name days later. His older brother, Charles Raymond, was five years old and welcomed his little brother gleefully. It would fifteen years later before sister, Marilyn Grace, made her debut.

This small unincorporated South Georgia town is located about eight miles west of Waycross, Georgia and those who lived there thought it about the best place anyone could live. The three stores at that time were, Spence, Tyre's and Uncle Joe's, who offered a variety of goods to the community. Folks were still feeling the effects of the Great Depression, so few owned automobiles. Waresboro did have its own Post Office and mail came twice a day by train, which made it convenient for its three hundred plus residents.

The Atlantic Coastline trains came roaring down the tracks day and night. It sounded as if they were coming right through the house, causing the windows to rattle and shake. One could hear the engineer blow the whistle miles away. In earlier years, Waresboro was the county seat of Ware County, but that changed when Waycross became a booming railroad town.

There wasn't a traffic light in the town, just a blinking caution light. The caution light was to warn drivers of an extremely sharp curve along side of the railroad tracks. Late at night cars passing through on their way to and from Waycross, unaware of this sharp turn in the road, often crashed. Wrecks happened when the driver came upon the curve driving too fast. The blinking light still blinks today.

There were only two churches; Methodist and Church of God. Pentecost came to the area and held services under a brush arbor. A mighty revival swept those parts and the Church of God was organized in August 1921, by Reverend Henry J. Murphy with the following eight members: Addie McDonald Holton (Kelland's great-grandmother), Eustace McDonald (Kelland's great uncle), Isabel Berry Jeffords (Kelland's mother), Mary Booth, Rebecca Booth, Corine Booth, Vara Rigdon and Lizzie Davis. The new church held services in Park Pavillian until 1922 when a Tabernacle was built on land donated by heirs of the Jeffords Family.

In 1934, the Tabernacle was torn down when a wood frame church was built on the same site. The Waresboro church is one of the oldest churches in the area. Even though it never became a large church, its influence was felt throughout that region. One could always boast that it was the largest church in town.

Many noted preachers filled the pulpit, which included General Overseer, State Overseer, Evangelists, and local pastor. Back then, there was no electricity, running water, or any of the modern conveniences like we know today. Kerosene lamps hung on walls while members of the congregation stood around the old pump organ and sang songs that lifted the souls of men. An old pot-bellied wood stove furnished heat for the building. But, the power of God was real. Many were convicted and experienced old time religion. Hearts were cleansed, sins forgiven, and revival spread from house to house.

Later, as the church grew in size, pastors modernized the church building with electricity, gas heaters, and updated church pews. In 1954, church growth continued when the Waresboro congregation built their first parsonage. In 1962, three Sunday School rooms were added for additional space. Expansion in 1968 was further realized with the purchase of a town lot to relocate and build a new church. Today, an air-conditioned lovely brick church is home to the Waresboro congregation. It stands as a testimony to the faithfulness of its membership. Through the years, it served as a lighthouse to the community and a reminder of those whose sacrifice kept the vision.

Over the years, the Waresboro Church of God congregation has seen a number of their own called and sent out to become some of the

Church of God's most successful church leaders. With the loving support from family and church, these individuals answered the call. They have made a difference in the world. We will never know just how much, but thank God for their obedience.

Ministers out of the Waresboro Church of God include:

Maggie Jeffords: Missionary/Evangelist, Bible Teacher

Eustace McDonald: Pastor, State and General Official-Church of God of Prophecy

Kelland Jeffords: Evangelist, Pastor, District Pastor, State Director of Youth and Christian Education-Georgia, State Council, State Youth Board, State Trustee, State Evangelism Board-Georgia

Rodney Jeffords: Evangelist, Pastor, Bible Teacher, State Council, State Overseer

Larry Hughes: Evangelist, Pastor, State Youth and Christian Education Director

E. Lamar McDaniel: Evangelist, Pastor, Missionary, Educator, Founder of European Bible Seminary in Germany, State Council, State Youth Board, Cluster Elder – Maryland

David Davis: Missionary – Guam, USA

In his preschool years, Kelland would often go to school with big brother, Raymond, and sing for the class, student body, or as just an individual. He would stand on a soda crate or box to be seen and heard. His blonde white hair and blue eyes made him a handsome little boy. They loved to hear him sing and he loved singing for them. His winning smile and cute personality made him a natural performer. Raymond called him an *entertainer*. He always had a word and smile for everyone.

This was the forerunner of what was to come. His singing and entertaining style only got better as he got older. Family reunions, parties, church gatherings, and school happenings gave him a chance to perform. People loved to hear him sing and he loved showing off his talents for them.

Kelland had a sense of humor. If there was something going on, you could be assured he was in the midst of it. He liked to have fun. He was likable. He loved people and people loved him. He made people feel good about themselves. He was compassionate. He was optimistic. He could always see the good in any situation. His thinking was positive. Everyone loved Kelland.

Finally, brethren, whatsoever things are true, whatsoever things are honest, whatsoever things are just, whatsoever things are pure, whatsoever things are lovely, whatsoever things are of good report; if there be any virtue, and if there be any praise, think on these things Philippians 4: 8

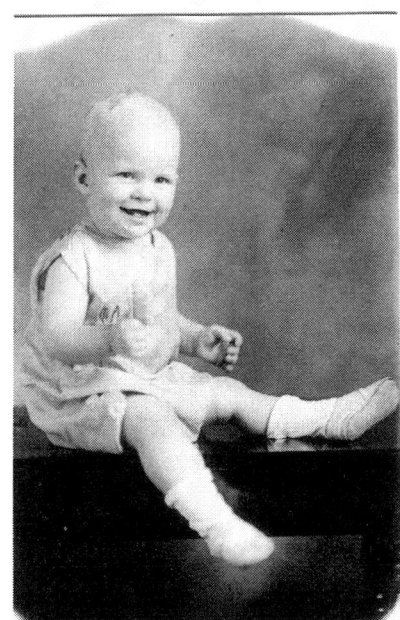

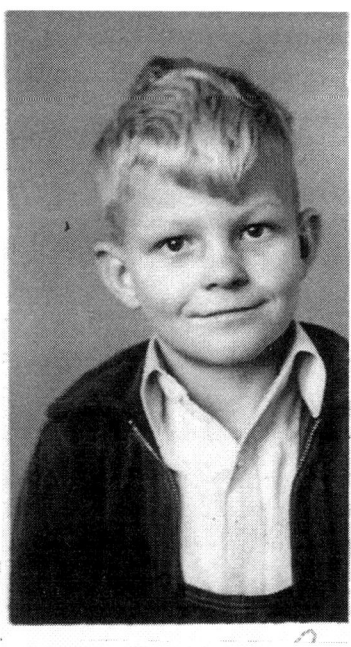

Kelland-11 months old

Kelland-little boy

Isabel, Raymond, Kelland

Kelland - a Young Lad

Marilyn-Aunt Maggie Jeffords   Marilyn and Kelland

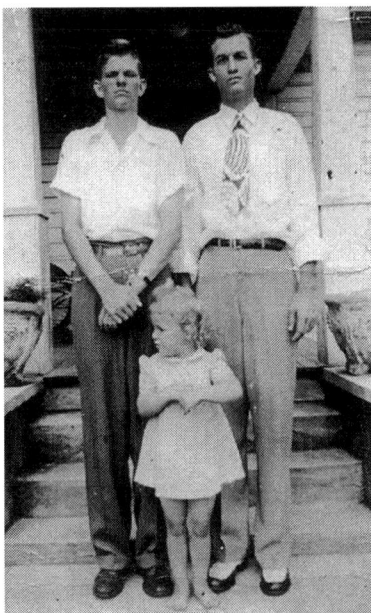

Kelland, Raymond, Marilyn

**Jeffords Grocery and Post Office
Waresboro, Georgia
Isabel Jeffords, Postmistress**

The Old Church in Waresboro, GA

MEMORABLE TRIBUTES FROM FAMILY AND FRIENDS

MEMORIES OF MY BROTHER

KELLAND JEFFORDS

It was around 1946 when I really can remember my brother Kelland. He was fifteen years old when I was born. My earliest remembrances of him was playing hide-and-go-seek with me, and also chasing me around the yard. He would jump over the yard fence, and with me being three years old, I had to go out the gate. Those were fun-filled times for me.

After his junior year in high school, he and a friend attended the Florida State Campmeeting. Both he and Rudolph McDaniel got saved while there. I was little and didn't understand all that was going on, but at the end of that summer, Kelland left home to go to Sevierville, Tennessee. At Bible Training School (BTS), he finished his senior year in high school. I was glad to have my brother back home in Waresboro.

After working that summer, he was off again to Lee College in Cleveland, Tennessee. He was always going and coming. I was the nosy little sister full of questions for him. But, he was kind and always had time for me. His activities included working in Waycross at H. C. Kress Company 5 & 10, J.C.Penny Company, or to the Georgia State Camp-meeting in Doraville, Georgia.

His career at J.C.Penny Company as a shoe salesman looked promising. Store Manager M.C. Thomas was grooming him for a future position. Kelland was good at his job. He loved people and people loved him. His enthusiasm was evident to those who worked with him. He earned the title as "shoe salesman of the year". Wow! He felt the call to ministry gnawing away at him inside. His job was going well and he loved doing what he was doing. But, there was something missing and he knew he had to go back to school and get himself prepared for what God had called him to do....PREACH!

He had been going back and forth to Jesup, Georgia dating Nelia. That year he had bought a new blue Chevrolet and was now facing a decision. Nelia was going to Lee College following her high school graduation. What was Kelland going to do? Would he keep working? After much prayer, Kelland decided to quit his job and return to Lee College.

While at Lee in 1950-51, he sang with the Messenger's Quartet traveling to churches, ministering in song. During Spring break, their tour of churches included Waycross, Georgia area and stayed at our house in Waresboro. I can remember sitting on quartet members' laps. What a thrill it was and such an enjoyable visit. I was so proud of my big brother!

I was eight years old when Kelland and Nelia got married in July, 1951. First, they began their ministry by evangelizing and would come stay at our house in between revivals. I could never keep up with them as their ministry kept them busy. It was an exciting time for me to be able to go and be in church with them whenever possible.

I remember well when they went to Albany, Georgia and began the East Albany Church of God. I thought it was cool worshipping under a tent. The ladies would make chicken dinners to sell for the church. Kelland would deliver the dinners to businesses and take me with him. I felt like a big girl. Kelland loved his little sister.

When Kelland and Nelia went to Griffin to pastor in 1956, I was thirteen years old. One of the highlights of my growing teens was when Kelland and Nelia took me to stay with them in the summertime. I looked forward to being with their group of young people. It was a time of spiritual growth for me to be involved with them in worship. The social atmosphere helped me to grow socially as well. I felt privileged to have had the opportunity. They treated like one of their own children.

Kelland was a person that loved people. He loved pastoring all people. He would visit hospitals, nursing homes, jails, businesses, and in homes. Sometimes he would take me along. I loved the time with him and it was a special for me.

As his sister, I felt that my brother was a mentor to me. He showed me the love of God through ministering to people. He was special. He was one of a kind.

Kelland's family, Nelia, Dianne, Keith and Danita, were all special and opened their home to many people....young people, ministers, and the like. He never expected his church members to do something that he wouldn't do himself. He used his personal car to bring people to church. When I got old enough I would help out by driving them home. Kelland was not selfish or self-centered. He always put others first.

While pastoring the Palace Street Church at Griffin, Kelland had a daily radio broadcast on station W.K.E.U. It was heard by thousands and most successful. One morning while preaching, a fire broke out in the station. Smoke was coming through the heater vents, around closed doors, and windows. It was a monster fire that completely destroyed the radio station. The radio personnel, along with Kelland, had to run out of the building for safety. The only thing that was not burned up in the fire was Kelland's bible. After the fire, he was known as the 'hell fire and brimstone' preacher. Isn't God good?

When he came home to Waresboro for a visit, he told my parents of victorious happenings about the church, pastor friends, and family. He was so uplifting and encouraging. My parents rejoiced and felt good because he never complained when he came for a visit. He always shared good news.

He loved the Church of God. Kelland was loved by all. Everybody loved Kelland. Everyone enjoyed his wit and humor. He was loyal. All ages loved to be around Kelland to listen to his encouraging words.

He was devoted to family; his mom, dad, brother Raymond, and little sister Marilyn. He loved his roots where he grew up. He used to say, "Waresboro, Georgia was the center of the universe". He loved his heritage of family, church, and love of God most of all.

It was heart breaking to see his health fail him. There were good days and bad days, but his desire to serve the church and preach was ever present. His heart to minister to the people was strong until the very end. The church people and family loved him unconditionally; they were with him until the end.

What a *'special'* brother the Lord gave me. After all these years I still miss him. One day we will all be together again. I have been so blessed.

Marilyn Jeffords O'Steen

BETTIE LOU JEFFORDS

Wife of Charles Raymond Jeffords (1923-2006)

Kelland was 14yrs. old when Raymond and I were married. Raymond told me stories of earlier times when Kelland and he were young boys. Raymond was always protective of his little brother and liked to show him off.

Raymond was five years old when Kelland was born. He had gotten a hatchet for his birthday and anxious to see if it really could chop wood. He decided to try it out and had gone to the woodpile chopping away when someone came to tell him that he had a new baby brother. October 26th was a 'special' day to him because that was the date he became a BIG brother. He was so proud that he now had a little brother. That pride was evident throughout their lifetime. It didn't take long for the bond between them to develop. He would tell everyone how thrilled he was because now they were a family of four.

Raymond described him as being energetic, full of mischief, talkative, but quite personable. He loved taking him to school and arranging for him to sing for the class. It became a regular thing for Kelland to go with Raymond and 'show off' in front of a few, or many, depending on the occasion. The classmates enjoyed Kelland's showmanship and wanted him to come back often.

When Kelland was about five or six, he would sneak out of church when everyone knelt to pray. Back then, the prayers were loud and long; much too long for a little boy to sit still and remain quiet. One night he tried to slip out when his dad caught his shirttail and pulled him back to the seat. Kelland loudly protested and said to his dad, "you are supposed to pray with your eyes closed." Dad Jeffords responded, "the Bible tells us to watch and pray." Needless to say that stopped the slipping out for some time.

Raymond started working for the Atlantic Coast Line Railroad when he was seventeen. His job was to relieve agents and operators for their vacations. This area of work took him all over Southern Georgia and North Florida. In between jobs he would come home. Kelland was getting ready for school on this morning, and thinking that Raymond was asleep, he was quietly combing his hair in front of the mirror. He was taking great pains to get every hair in place while admiring himself at the same time. He suddenly said, "you know who is good looking this morning? You are…. that's who." Raymond lifted his head from the pillow and surprised Kelland by saying, "you don't say". Kelland was much chagrined! Charging out of the room, he left for school.

Raymond was a telegraph operator for the railroad and now in a permanent position in Waycross. Oftentimes the boys and girls would hitch a ride into town and go to a movie or some other event. They came into the depot office to let Raymond know that when he got off work at midnight, they would like a ride home. When Kelland was in his mid-teens, he came into Raymond's office one night to let him know he would need to ride home with him.

After Kelland went outside to wait for him, Raymond thought of something he wanted to tell Kelland. As Raymond got to the front door of the depot office he saw Kelland lighting a cigarette. Just then Kelland saw Raymond. Before Raymond could utter a word Kelland said, "if you tell mama you lied." After Raymond got through preaching to him that put an end to Kelland's smoking.

There was always much love and respect between the brothers. Throughout their life, Kelland knew Raymond's love transcended whatever disagreements there might be. Also, Raymond took pride in whatever Kelland was doing. When he worked for J.C.Penny, attended Bible Training School, enrolled at Lee College, and when he launched his ministry, he knew that his big brother was praying for him and wishing him success.

Not only love of kinship, but love of God, which is the deepest kind of love. When Kelland started working for the Lord, he was always interested in where he was, what he was doing, and always held him up in prayer. There was never a time, as his BIG BROTHER, that he wasn't there for him.

Bettie Lou Jeffords
Waresboro, Georgia

Chapter 2

Growing Up Years

During high school years, Kelland was active in sports. The high school was too small for a football team, so the main sporting event was basketball. Waresboro High's 'Purple Martin' Basketball Team was second to none and enjoyed many winning seasons. It was the popular thing to be a member of the 'Purple Martin' basketball team.

The summer following his junior year in high school, Aunt Maggie Jeffords persuaded Kelland to go to the Wimauma Florida Camp-meeting. She told him many pretty girls would be there. He would have the opportunity to meet numerous new friends. There would lots of good singing. The more she talked the more she aroused his interest. She knew if he got to camp-meeting, he would get saved. After much talking, and praying, he agreed to go. He and his friend, Rudolph McDaniel, packed their bags and were off to the Florida Camp Meeting. Little did he know that this trip would change his life forever.

Sure enough, he was gloriously saved, baptized in the Holy Ghost, and received his call to ministry at the 1946 Florida Camp-meeting. He never questioned his call to ministry because that night of his conversion and Holy Ghost baptism was unmistakable. He was slain in the spirit for more than an hour. When he came to, he was told he had been preaching under the anointing to a crowd of people gathered around him. The call became even more definite as time went on.

It was a time of rejoicing when he returned home to Waresboro. His parents were thrilled about his conversion and call to the ministry, but voiced concern about getting back with his unsaved friends. They were probably right. If he finished his senior year at Waresboro High, he would be back on the varsity basketball team, playing baseball, going to movies, and dating sinner girls. These types of activities were considered wrong and the church stood against such things. Mom and Dad Jeffords didn't want to take the chance of him going back with his "old worldly crowd."

By late summer, Kelland was on a bus going to Sevierville, Tennessee. He would complete his senior year of high school at Bible Training School (BTS). Coming from the flat woods of South Georgia to the majestic mountains of Eastern Tennessee was an awesome experience for a seventeen-year-old young man. The great Smokey Mountains was quite a difference from the Okefenokee Swamp area known as the "land of trembling earth."

The geographic difference was amazement enough, but there was the cultural shock, too. Dozens of old men sitting on the streets of downtown Sevierville 'whittling sticks of wood' and chewing wads of tobacco was a new sight for him. He had never seen such since no one in his family smoked, dipped, or chewed tobacco. He laughed and laughed as he watched those mountaineers contentedly doing their thing. He tiptoed carefully to avoid puddles of tobacco juice on the sidewalk. This was quite a contrast from growing up in Ware County.

The years 1946-47 at BTS did not disappoint him. He made many life-long friends in this new environment. The Christian atmosphere that prevailed on campus helped him grow spiritually. It provided a chance to develop and further use his musical talents. And, perhaps the thing he enjoyed most was playing on the baseball and basketball teams. In his book, *Bennie*, author Bennie S. Triplett states on page 77 that "Kelland Jeffords was a good second baseman". He was actively involved in campus activities, which also helped the year to pass swiftly. He completed his senior year of high school and looked forward to college.

He and some friends heard about a revival at the "snake handling church" not far from Sevierville. Their curiosity got the best of them and decided to go and see for themselves. Although apprehensive about the idea of handling snakes, off they went. The church service was in full swing. People were shouting, singing to the top of their voices, and acted like any ordinary Pentecostal church where people informally worshipped.

"But where are the snakes," he thought. After the service was going with fever-pitch excitement, out came the snake. A man assigned to bring them to and from church had a large snake in a box. People began to come forward and line-up across the church in front of the altar. Kelland particularity noticed one slender girl, rather timid in nature. Somehow, she had been pulled into the line. She was fervently praying with eyes closed and hands raised.

The snake started being passed at the beginning of the line and making his way from one to the other. Kelland was looking, sitting on the edge of his seat, not wanting to miss one thing during this never seen before spectacle. The snake got to the young lady. She stepped back and called out in shrill voice, "Hello, HELLO, pass him to ole Carlo." So, the snake got passed on to Carlo.

Never again did Kelland go to a snake handling church service. That was enough for him. He remembered well the story of Rev. John L. Stevens who visited a church where the snakes were being handled. One of the brethren tried to get Brother Stevens to take part, but he replied, "I perceive that the snake has been handled enough."

In 1948, the Bible Training School moved to Cleveland, Tennessee and became known as Lee College. Kelland made the move with BTS enrolling as a freshman. There was much excitement among the student body. An expanded curriculum and larger campus was sure to attract more students. He was happy to be a part of the growing educational department of the church.

Returning home to Waresboro, Georgia for the summer, he made plans to attend the 1949 Georgia Camp Meeting in Doraville, Georgia the week of July 4th. It was always a glorious time of spiritual refreshing. Thousands of people came from across Georgia and neighboring states to attend the annual event. There were hundreds of young people, too. This was the place to get acquainted with each other and, hopefully, find a potential mate. Many courtships were begun around the 'water fountain" at the Georgia Campground.

I was one of the youth that attended the 1949 Georgia Camp-Meeting. I had met a nice young man that summer and thought it might lead into a relationship. But, I still had my senior year in high school to finish and that took precedence over relationships. Kelland had met a young lady and, according to her, fell madly in love. They saw each other quite regularly during camp-meeting. She introduced me, but I brushed it off as she said, "he was so interested in her."

After a week of 'oohing and ahhing' over boys I had met, I went home to South Georgia and back to making plans for my last year in high school, but remembering the good times I enjoyed at camp-meeting. Oh, this year at dear ole' Jesup High was going to be the best yet. I was making plans for all the things I wanted to do in my senior year. It would be a blast!

Toward the end of summer I received a letter. It must have been divine providence that the letter was delivered to the right address because it was addressed to 'Miss Lelia Flowers'. I was shocked as I looked at the return address to see who had written me. It was from Kelland Jeffords. My heart was racing with excitement. I was flattered, but surprised that he was writing me.

Nelia Flowers
Senior High School Picture

Anxiously, I opened the letter. It was sweet, short, and right to the point. He wrote that when he met me earlier at camp-meeting he wanted to date me, but since I was dating someone else he didn't want to intrude. I had made an impression on him and thought I was lots of fun. He would like to come to Jesup for a visit. Wow!

My sister, Aletha Flowers Waters, tells how it was for her and my family when they met Kelland Jeffords for the first time.

The Flowers Family Meets Kelland Jeffords

It was one of those lazy, hazy summer evenings in mid-August. The cows had come down the lane lowing, with cowbells chiming their tune – an everyday ritual. Dad was across the road putting the cows in their stalls and I, with all the inquisitiveness of a ten year old, was watching – but not keeping an eye on the cows. I was looking at the old dirt road, because any minute now, Nelia's new boyfriend would arrive! I liked to hang around and watch her succession of boyfriends but more, I enjoyed watching Daddy's reaction to them. Now, that is another story!

The moment arrived! A shinny light green Dodge car stopped and out stepped a skinny young man, neat as a pin, with a shock of Billy Graham type hair all neatly combed and in perfect place. His most pleasant and aggressive personality seemed to reach out farther than his body. With an outstretched hand and a most confident million dollar smile, Kelland Jeffords met the Talmadge Flowers family. It was instant success! Daddy could always judge a person and he judged this young man A-O-K. So, there were no fireworks today out of daddy. Was I a little disappointed? Maybe…but not for long. We were soon mesmerized with this new boyfriend and his tales of "W-a-a-z-boro". We were hearing about a "Mayberry" before there was one on TV. What characters they were: Uncle Orbie, Uncle Eustace, Bill Hargraves, 'Thee' Paul, and "Little Kenny"….now those were some stories. Entertaining and funny were the hallmarks of Kelland's stories---nothing derogatory – just comical stuff.

I guess we all fell in love with Kelland Jeffords that day. He had sold himself, but then he was a natural salesman. It was no wonder that he had won many awards selling shoes at J. C. Penny's in Waycross, Georgia. There was an openness, a honesty, a pure, nothing hidden feeling one got about Kelland. There was a goodness about him that was to be with him all his life. He truly was a delight to be around. He had won our hearts and we loved him as our own. We learned to love all the Jeffords family; good people that seem like our family to this day.

We continued to look forward to Nelia s dates with Kelland. He always had some good stories to tell. Our life revolved around Blanton Grove Church of God and we were delighted to hear church stories. There were those about his Aunt Mag and her great faith, her involvement with our first missionaries, about Bishop Arthur Moore the great Methodist bishop whose wife was a friend and relative. Such a rich heritage! I'm sure this all contributed to Kelland Jeffords being the person that he was: *truly bigger than life.*

Aletha Flowers Waters
Jesup, Georgia

Kelland came for the visit, then, another and another. We continued our courtship through my senior year and into the next summer. As I made plans to enter college at Lee, so did he. But, he thought we should test our relationship and not see each other. I agreed. I had just turned sixteen in April and graduated in May 1950. He was five years older and had been to Lee College previously.

I had a yen for adventure. Going to Lee was going to be fun and this was just the beginning for me. Meeting new friends and getting mesmerized with college activities was the way to go. So, I did just that. I sang in and played for a ladies trio, was a cheerleader for the freshman basketball team, member of the drama club, and the list goes on. I became more and more involved as the months passed. I loved being there!

Before we realized it, we were going home for Christmas break. Semester exams were over. Whew! Now, I'm saying 'good-by' to the friends I had made my first semester at college. So much activity and so many friends had given me a fulfilled four-and-a-half months of college life. How could I ask for anything more?

Kelland wanted to see me during the holidays. I, reluctantly, agreed. After all, we had not dated for over four months. It was a little strange, but he came and after much talking, I complied with his decision that the waiting period was sufficient for both of us. He reasoned that his love had been tested long enough. He didn't want to lose me. So, for four weeks while on Christmas break, we saw each other quite often. We picked up right where we left off before going to Lee. He was convinced our relationship was for real and asked me to marry him. Now, my head was really in a spin. I didn't want to lose him either. This was happening so fast. Eventually I said 'yes', and we returned second semester as an engaged couple.

While at Lee, Kelland was involved in several activities including music and sports. Though he played on the basketball and baseball teams, he still found time to sing with the Messenger's Quartet. In 1950 there were several quartets groups on campus that would travel on weekends to churches singing and preaching. It gave students the opportunity to preach, to sing, plus build good public relations for the college. Also, from the offering received, it gave them spending money, which was sometimes much and sometimes not so much.

I looked forward to our dates when Kelland got back from a weekend of quartet traveling. If the offerings were good, I didn't have to pay for my food, tickets to concerts, etc. He always paid my way if he could afford it. Otherwise, I would pay. Both he and I were on a tight budget and had to watch how we spent money. We usually split the cost while at college.

It was a good year as I look back to all the good times we had. We made many friends that remain even to this day. I'm convinced that two people's lives don't cross per chance. Somewhere down the road you will meet that person again. That was the case of the many, many friends we made that year at Lee College. I wouldn't trade my experience if I could.

Prayer: God grant us your *Favor* each day. Grace is the "unmerited favor" and comes from you only. We need your love and guidance as we start our lives together. In Jeremiah 1:12 *"Then said the Lord unto me, Thou hast well seen: for I will hasten my word to perform it."*

Only you can give us *"favor"* with man, and thereby we will be advantaged, with your help in accomplishing the things that you want us to do. It is with this desire I pray. Amen

MEMORABLE TRIBUTES FROM FAMILY AND FRIENDS

GROWING UP IN WARESBORO

Kelland and I grew up in the same area. He lived in the little town of Waresboro and I lived on a farm four miles out in the country. We attended the Waresboro High School together and played on the Purple Martin Basket ball team.

Mr. C.P. Hamilton, Agriculture teacher, organized a F.F.A. (Future Farmers of America) quartet and both Kelland and I sang in it. We traveled over large areas of the state winning in competition events. Since it was a small high school (only 26 in graduating class), our conspicuous activities made us two of the most popular boys in school.

When our Junior-Senior banquet came around, he and I were able to take the two prettiest and most popular girls to the banquet. Kelland borrowed his brother Raymond's, car, picked me up and we drove to Millwood to get the girls. Being "dressed to our teeth" and escorting the prettiest girls, as young "whipper-snapper teenagers", we thought we had really arrived.

That summer Kelland and my cousin, Rudolph McDaniel, went to the Florida Campmeeting in search of 'girls', but instead, both found "salvation." They returned saved boys and I felt very awkward around them. I must have acted very strangely. Kelland said to me, "Lamar, don't be afraid or run from me. I'm the same Kelland, only I'm saved now." Regardless of his explanation, I still didn't feel comfortable around him because I was not saved. I understand now that it was the conviction of the Holy Spirit on me.

He and I had become very close friends, playing on the ball team, singing in the High School quartet, spending much time at each others' houses. We also attended the same church together, sitting back and laughing and enjoying any peculiar happenings at the church services. If there were none, he'd create something. He'd set next to me with his hand to his mouth and whisper "watch Aunt Mag'", or, "keep your eye on Uncle Orbie, or you'll miss it." Sure enough, Aunt Mag, who was a peculiarity in herself, would throw her hands into the air and praise the Lord, or speak in tongues. Perhaps Uncle Orbie would "twist/twitch his nose" which he was good at. Then Kelland would begin to giggle and say, "I told you so, keep your eyes on them".

Obviously, as unsaved church teenage boys, we were not there to worship, but rather to be entertained. One time he got some humorous thing going and we couldn't stop laughing. If our parents had seen us, we would have been in trouble. To keep from disturbing the service with my subdued laughter, I laid down on the bench to hide, but fell off onto the floor, which really caused a disturbance. We made everything fun.

Now he is saved and I am not. Then, off to Bible Training School in Sevierville, Tennessee he went and left me home. But in April, just before my graduation, I got saved. When he returned from Bible School, the pastor of the Waresboro Church of God organized a church quartet and we both sang in it. It became quite a good singing group.

Each of our conversions to Christ really shook up our High School. None of the other students confessed the Lord, or professed to be born again believers. Since both of us were very popular, it was the talk of the whole school that Kelland and Lamar had gotten "religion".

One of our real "worldly" high school friends was trying to explain how Kelland had gotten saved and was so changed, didn't know much religious language, so he finally blurted out, "he's got the shimmy-she-wobbles".

Later, and through the years, as classmates we came together occasionally for school reunions. All of the other classmates have held us in highest esteem and appreciation. Thank God, numbers of them have since confessed the Lord as Saviour.

Both of us went on to Bible School to prepare for ministry. Then our ways parted. Kelland was married to Nelia and did evangelistic and youth work. I married Ardys and went to Europe to do mission work. From time to time, our paths would cross and we were always able to pick up where we left off at the last meeting. There was always laughter, reminiscing and fun.

I did preach in his church from time to time, but our ministries were usually far from each other, but not too far to know and appreciate what the other was doing.

Rev. Dr. E. Lamar McDaniel, Baltimore, Maryland

TRIBUTE TO A FRIEND

By definition, the dictionary tells us that a friend is a companion, a supporter, and a colleague. In every sense of the word, Kelland Jeffords was a friend.

It all started at Lee College (now Lee University) when we were <u>friends as students.</u>

In 1950, Kelland and I shared playing basketball at Lee and forming a quartet called the *Messengers*. There were five of us. Kelland sang the second tenor or lead; I played the piano, did the arrangements and served as the preacher. On the weekends we would leave the campus and minister at various churches throughout the Southeast.

One special feature of our weekends was serving as a part of the popular all-night singing conventions of that era. These conventions featured all of the well-known professional groups, and we were involved as "fill ins" between the headliners to provide a break. These conventions were very important to us because we were paid $100 to participate. When this was added to our Sunday offerings, it meant everything to us as college students.

On occasion the five of us, as the *Messengers*, would visit high schools to minister. We would play an exhibition basketball game against the local high school teams. During half time we would present a thirty-minute concert complete with testimonies and invitation for students to accept Christ. This proved to very effective but would not be acceptable today because of the secular laws regarding church and state.

We were <u>friends in ministry.</u> In our ministry days after Lee, we both pastored in the greater Atlanta, Georgia, area. During the Sunday School contest era, we were friendly rivals in the attendance drives.

To say the least, Kelland and Nelia made a very impressionable team and God gave them success in every pastoral venture.

Most of all, however, we were <u>friends as disciples of Christ</u> called of God to do the work of the ministry. We shared ideas, plans and outreaches. His enthusiasm, positive attitude and deep desire to make a "mark" for Christ were all contagious and inspired to all whom he ministered.

Now, because of my deep personal appreciation for our lifetime relationship, I am honored to share this tribute to his memory – Kelland was a friend!

Paul L. Walker, Ph.D.
Secretary General Church of God International
Cleveland, TN

Senior Pastor Emeritus
Mount Paran Church of God
Atlanta, GA

Dr. Terrell McBrayer
821 McPherson St.
Bremen, Georgia 30110

A TRIBUTE TO THE LATE REVEREND KELLAND JEFFORDS

Kelland was a special person, and remains so in my memory bank; he was special in many ways, a great person, a great friend, and a great preacher!

My association with Kelland goes back to Lee College Days when we were roommates. He was a pleasant, handsome person, with a great sense of humor, but he needed me to scratch his back, and that is one thing I'm too lazy to do well! I neglect my own back, and I am sure I was a disappointment to Kelland in the back-scratching role.

Kelland was interested in people. During our college days, he talked a lot about his home church, and his home town, referring often to people by name, and commenting on their Christian life and the human condition. But, he talked about Nelia more than any one else or anything else!

Kelland preached his first sermon during his courting days at the Bremen Church of God, and he did very well in his first of many sermons. He had a great style of preaching; from his descriptive delivery, he could cause his audience to see images. His sense of humor was contagious. We all got a real kick out of his common practice of pausing when he had a mental block, to say, "Nelia...?".

Teaming with his energetic and talented wife, Nelia, their ministry has affected the lives of thousands across Georgia and other areas. Particularly significant was their ministry to the youth when they served in the important position as Youth Director of Georgia.

I especially appreciated his friendship with my late brother, Rev. David Columbus McBrayer. They shared a close brotherly bond.

The memories of Kelland are very much alive, and I cherish the belief that he and David are now enjoying the blessings of Heaven.

Kelland fought a good fight for the Kingdom, and we cherish the hope of that great reunion day when we can join together to renew auld acquaintance and hear him sing again. Maybe David can carry a tune then also.

--by, R. Terrell McBrayer, Sr., April 22, 2002

Jeffords Grocery - Post Office
Waresboro, Georgia

Kelland and Lamar

Waresboro's Purple Martin Basketball Team

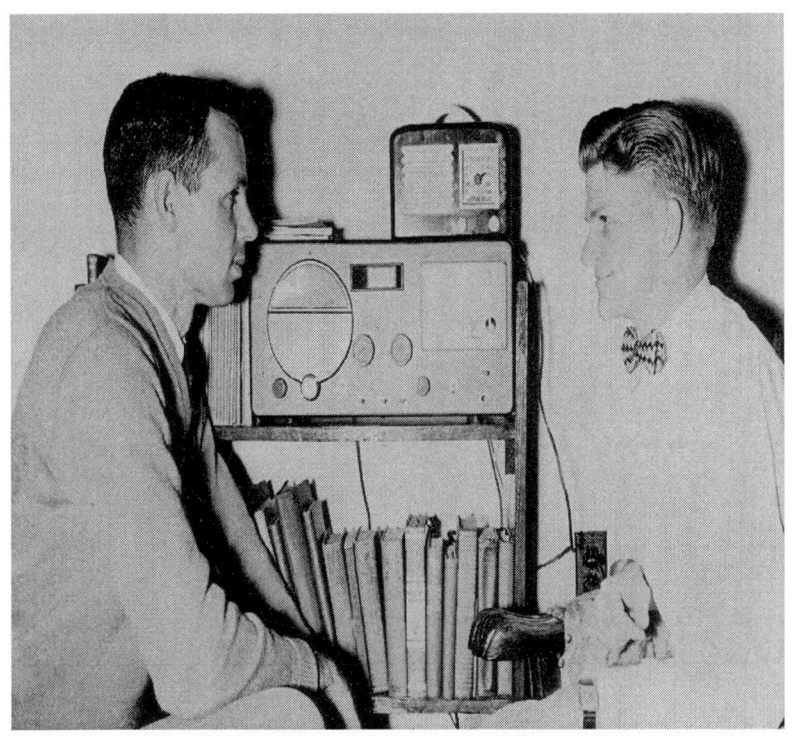

Cousin Jackie And Kelland

Standing: Kelland Jeffords- R.L.Newman-Lavoy Johnson
Seated: Paul L. Walker-Bruce Bennett

Chapter 3

Love and Marriage

Again, it was home for summer break. What a year! What a glorious year! He was now busy making future plans. Instead of returning to Lee College for the fall semester, he felt the time had come for him to enter full-time ministry. He went to Georgia State Camp Meeting the summer of 1951. This was the order in which plans for ministry were made. A young minister would first start his ministry as an evangelist. After some successful revivals, the young evangelist hoped he would be in demand. Pastors would be calling and asking them to come to their church. That was the prayer and hope of every young minister.

Kelland thought it best to begin his ministry as a married evangelist. He knew I had planned to return to Lee College in the fall, but those plans never materialized. Being the persuasive young man that he was, we started making plans for a summer wedding. We didn't have time to plan a big wedding, so a smaller affair would have to do.

With help from all the family plans got underway. The date was set for July 29, 1951. My home church, Blanton's Grove Church of God, was an old white clapboard church and really not suitable, I thought. The inside looked even worse. So, the second thought was to have a garden wedding at my parent's home. The lush green lawn and landscaped gardens made it picture perfect for that important day. The large country home sat in the middle of a small pecan orchard. The big trees with sprawling branches always provided a cool breeze and shade in summer. The spacious yard made a beautiful setting for the late July nuptials.

Work began and everyone joined in to make our "special day" a memorable one. All the plans came together and the day finally arrived. Amid the flurry of activities, we didn't expect inclement weather to be a problem. What a problem it caused. The rain came down in buckets it seemed. For an outside wedding that just would not do to have the wedding party and guests getting soaked. So, we had no option but to move the wedding inside the house.

We did just that. The capacious living room was adequate for the wedding. It was a very large room and made a handsome setting for the happy occasion. Dozens and dozens of guests arrived dressed in their beauteous attire for the summer garden wedding. Though it was disappointing to them that plans had to be changed at the last minute because of the July showers, it was a charming affair at the Flowers country home. It was beautiful! The lavish reception following the ceremony was equally as elegant.

After a short honeymoon to Florida, we arrived back in Jesup with little time to prepare for our first revival. We packed up Kelland's blue Chevrolet and off on our trip to a town located somewhere in southwest Georgia. This was new territory for us, but we found our way to Donaldson, Georgia where the pastor greeted us with a warm friendly welcome.

John 15:7 "If ye abide in me, and my words abide in you, ye shall ask what ye will, and it shall be done unto you."

Father, we ask that you go before us and prepare hearts for a great revival. We believe your word for it is in thy name we ask. Amen

Kelland Jeffords
1950-51
Lee College – Cleveland, TN.

Nelia Flowers
Lee College – Cleveland, Tennessee

Flowers Family Country Home
(a rare occurance of snow)
Jesup, Georgia

Kelland and Nelia Wedding   Dad & Mom Flowers

**Blanton Grove Church of God
Nelia, Mother Flowers, Virginia
Aletha Flowers**   **Nelia and Kelland**

Jeffords family at 50th wedding anniversary
Marilyn, Dad, Mom, Raymond, Bettie Lou, Nelia, Kelland

Raymond and Bettie Lou   **Marilyn and David**

Chapter 4

Ministerial Journey

We began the revival at the Donaldsonville Church of God. It was an uncomfortable and humid August. Sizzling temperatures soared into the nineties and was it ever hot! The church was not air-conditioned. In spite of the intense heat, people came to hear the young preacher and his wife sing and preach; *so did the gnats!* God gave revival regardless of these minor hindrances.

The congregation was made up mostly of cotton farmers. It was a beautiful site to see fields and fields of white fluffy cotton ready for harvest. The people came to church late because they worked in the fields until dark. Thus, the night services began at 'dark-thirty.' However, we were grateful for their faithfulness to come night after night to revival. Many souls were saved, uplifted, and encouraged. Considering the circumstances, we felt pleased in our hearts that we had done what we could. They were a blessed group of people. We never forgot our 'first' revival.

Another small church in North Georgia was struggling and having difficulty just paying the bills. We didn't know about their problem. The pastor was not in the best of health to add to their miserable status. In fact, they were trying to starve him out by withholding their tithe.

We prayed for revival. Oh, how we prayed! Kelland and I agreed in prayer that we would be able to reach the people, and reach them we did. The church was filled with people each night as we prayed, sang, and preached. People repented for their disobedience and began seeking a closer walk. Heaven came down with a refreshing touch of His glory. Love filled hearts where hatred had been. It was a different congregation than when we came.

There was an outbreak of influenza in the county. All public places like theatre's, schools, ballgames, had cancelled their events. Churches were the last to be closed. The county had been quarantined and we had to leave quickly. Before we left, Kelland felt that he should give the ailing pastor the offering that had been given us, so he did. What was the statistics of this revival? Only heaven knows and that is all that matters.

Kelland called the pastor where our next revival was scheduled and explained why we needed to come a week earlier than planned. He said, "Bro. Norris, an epidemic has broken out here and we're closing the revival. The revival was going great and now we have to leave. All public places were closed earlier but now they are closing the churches. This epidemic struck all over the 't**y' (his tongue got twisted when he started to say town and city at the same time)". We all burst out laughing and on the other end of the phone, the pastor was saying, "What did you say? What was that, Kelland?" At least we could find some humor amid the disappointment of the moment.

In those days revivals lasted sometimes two or more weeks. The longest revival we ever held was five weeks. A number of our revivals lasted four weeks straight. The revival would set the path of growth in the church to unprecedented heights. Sometimes we were in church for two and three months without a night off. We would go from one revival to the next.

After a year and a half on the evangelistic field, Kelland was ask to come to the Hemphill Avenue Church of God to serve as the assistant pastor. His success as an evangelist was noised about which made him a sought after young minister. After much prayer and fasting, he felt this would give him the opportunity to learn what he could about pastoral duties. The Hemphill Avenue church was the largest Church of God in the state of Georgia. He could learn much being mentored by Pastor Paulk who was known throughout the denomination as a model pastor.

We worked diligently while serving the Hemphill Avenue church. I assisted in the music program while Kelland was busy visiting the sick, shut-ins, follow up of newcomers, and whatever the pastor assigned him to do. We served enthusiastically! Once Kelland was giving a pep talk on how to grow a Sunday School. "One way we can grow," he stated, "is for every family to increase by one, or, if each lady has twins." The workers really laughed at his suggestion.

Kelland took time out of his daily routine to continue his education. He enrolled at Oglethorpe University in Atlanta, Georgia while on staff at the church at Hemphill Avenue. However, we left the church before he graduated. So many invitations to minister elsewhere were coming our way.

We loved the opportunity that was given us to serve as Assistant Pastor of the prestigious Hemphill Avenue Church of God. We had learned so much. The experience of working in a large church was worth more than we could have ever imagined, or afford to pay. After a year passed, Kelland felt it was time to leave this position. Isn't it amazing that you feel restless in the midst of such an ideal setting? There is a gnawing away inside you, a restlessness that the Lord wants you to work elsewhere. The Spirit is telling you to move on to other fields of labor. We were where everything was comfortable for us; a great congregation of lovely people. We should have been the most satisfied couple chosen to work with this great church and prominent pastor. It was an opportunity of a lifetime.

Hemphill Avenue Church of God

MEMORABLE TRIBUTES FROM FAMILY AND FRIENDS

North Georgia Church of God Executive Office

962 Parkside Walk Lane' Lawrenceville, GA 30043-7313

September 17, 2006

To Whom It May Concern:

In 1953, a young girl attended a revival service at the Hemphill Avenue Church of God in Atlanta, Georgia (now Mount Paran Central) and she experienced a glorious salvation experience and baptism in the Holy Ghost. The visiting evangelist for that revival was Reverend Lamar McDaniel.

She was from an un-churched family with alcohol abuse problems. Her mother and stepfather were quite upset that she wanted to attend such a radical church. But, because of the love and care extended by church members who made transportation to church possible, she was able to persuade her parents to allow her to attend. Not many months later the parents forced her out of their home and she moved in with grandparents. Soon after that trauma, a church family opened their home to her and she changed schools and moved in with them.

During the '50's, she led many young people to the Lord and was a very faithful church member. She was nurtured by Sunday School teachers, youth leaders and influential people God put in her life. She became very involved in youth activities and outreach.

Kelland K. Jeffords and Nelia were church staff personnel-extraordinaire! Nelia was a bubbly, highly energetic woman of God. Her charismatic personality was contagious. Her musical talents were outstanding. And, Kelland was a man of God who captured the loyalty of those who fell under his ministry. What a team they were!

Kelland had a way of making you feel special not only to God and the church, but to the family of God. He was an encourager. He demonstrated loyalty and commitment. He took time for people. He was a "people person". He modeled a Christian *life walk* and a faith in God and others.

That young girl who needed good role models - found such in Kelland and Nelia. I know, I was that girl.

I went on to Lee University, met and married a young man who later devoted himself to ministry. Over the years, I followed the ministries of Kelland as he and Nelia served in many different places and touched the lives of hundreds of young people; as well as the entire denomination. They were a ministry team.

They touched the life of this one young Atlanta girl and left an indelible print. They touched the lives of hundreds of other young men and women with pulpit ministry, gospel teaching, a gift of laughter, youth choirs and other musical involvements and just by the fact that they embraced them and genuinely loved them.

Their children reflect the same kind of commitment and love that has been handed down from the parents. Kelland was called home early in life. Nelia later married a man who had lost his ministry companion to an early death also; and, as God would have it, Lamar McDaniel and Nelia were wed and now they serve as partners in ministry.

How interesting it is that Pastor McDaniel had an impact in my life and then along came Pastor Jeffords, who also made a significant deposit in my life. The woman they loved and shared marriage and ministry is a person with whom I have maintained a bond and friendship over these now fifty-plus years. Wow - that sounds like a very long time.

Life has a way of coloring pages in our story that at the time seem unplanned. But, as we age and look back we see how God has had a hand in many areas of our lives that we just didn't see at the time. And, He allows us to meet, be influenced, and mentored by people whose relationship we cherish for a lifetime.

Such it is for me. Thanks to this former Youth Pastor who cared for a young, insignificant young girl and took time to pour into my life and encourage me with scripture and example.

He prayed for me. I trust he is looking down and is somehow pleased that I am just one of many whose life he touched - who loves God, loves the Church of God and remembers and respects his memory.

Respectfully,

Jackie T. Walker

Jackie T. Walker
State Director of Women's Ministries
North Georgia Church of God State Office

MEMORIES OF KELLAND JEFFORDS THAT WILL LIVE FOREVER

I first met Kelland Jeffords in 1946 at the Church of God Bible Training School, Sevierville, Tennessee. Kelland was finishing his last year of high school and I was a student in the Ministerial Division. He was a cheerful, vibrant young teenager full of life and excitement. He never grew tired or weary and his 'throttle' was always wide open.

Kelland had received God's call to the ministry, which he pursued with all diligence and commitment. After college, he was married to his life long helpmate, the beautiful talented teenager, Nelia Flowers, who became such a vital and tremendous part of this ministerial team.

After college years and a period of Evangelistic Ministry, I was now pastor of the Church of God in Rockmart, Georgia. I was fortunate to schedule Kelland and Nelia Jeffords, who were now in full-time Evangelism, for a revival. Both of them were very talented musically. Nelia was a very accomplished pianist and singer: Kelland was a talented singer. Their ministry in music, song, and message was greatly anointed of the Lord and we realized a spiritual harvest of souls.

I moved to Lawrenceville, Georgia in 1954, and became the pastor of the Lawrenceville Church of God. Again, I was able to schedule Kelland and Nelia for a revival in September 1955. This revival did not just continue for a week or two weeks, but continued the entire month of September. This was the revival which began the tremendous growth of the Lawrenceville Church. Recently, I attended the Senior Adult Fellowship in Lawrenceville and sat at the table with a man who was saved in that revival.

The people in Lawrenceville loved the Jeffords so much that they wanted them as their pastor when I moved to Macon, Georgia. However, they had made another commitment at the time.

After some years in the evangelistic work, God called Kelland and Nelia to pastor.   God used them to build strong congregations Kelland believed, as was our theme in earlier years, the Sunday School was the Church's greatest arm of Evangelism.   He was *greatest Sunday School pastor* I ever knew.

I recall a very pleasant and enjoyable experience with Kelland and Nelia.   It was in earlier days when *Singspiration Rallies* were scheduled in various areas of the state to introduce the new convention songbook. I was asked to travel with Kelland and Nelia into South Georgia for some of these rallies. I remember riding in the back seat of their little Volkswagen bug. Also, I was privileged to meet members of their families in Waresboro and Blanton Grove during the tour.

Kelland was an outstanding State Youth and Christian Education Director. I worked with him in many State Youth Camps, which were extremely successful. Kelland was hard to beat while playing softball and horseshoes.

I will always cherish the precious memories of our relationship. And, I look forward to that happy reunion which will last *eternally!*

Lewis Stover, Jr.
Retired Minister

Yet, the Bible tells us it is better "to obey is better than sacrifice". If one wants to walk in obedience with the Lord material things have little meaning. What a contented feeling to feel like you are doing just that…walking in obedience. Nothing else matters. When the Lord "directs our paths", he will lead you and prepare you for greater things ahead.

State Overseer, D.C. Boatwright asked Kelland to go into new fieldwork. He had two towns in mind….Manchester and Albany. The state would supplement us financially for six months. After much urging from the overseer, he accepted the call as a *church planter*. It was not financially advantageous for us to accept this new program. Back then, finances for the state and churches were limited. Why then were we accepting this new offer?

First, the overseer was his authority. If we are to be obedient to God, we also must submit to them that have rule over us. Kelland was never one to usurp his will over the will of those in authority over him. It was purely a step of *faith*. He wanted the Lord blessings on his life so he took the challenge.

We left Hemphill church and many friends behind. Therefore, we honestly felt we were doing God's will. We had many people praying for our ministry. We knew that this decision was no different. God is *faithful!* We trusted Him to direct us.

We found a lot to erect a tent. A one-bedroom house nearby would be our home for the next eighteen months. We referred to it as 'four rooms and a path'. After a blitz of advertising, we began the revival and organized the East Albany Church of God with eighteen members. A lot of good things, as well as hardships, came our way. Turner Air Force Base located nearby brought new families from many states to the area. We enjoyed them all as the worshipped with us and had good fellowship.

In the beginning we had some hard and difficult times. The church was struggling financially. While visiting my parents, Kelland was relating this need. My dad who wasn't a Christian at the time said,

"Kelland, I wouldn't waste my time with those dead beats. Why don't you just quit and tell them all to 'go to hell?"

Although we still worshipped in a tent, the church grew by leaps and bounds. Kelland's enthusiastic spirit never ceased. He loved working for the Kingdom of God and nothing excited him more than a sinner coming to Christ. He followed every lead whether by a visit to the church or someone giving him the name of a friend, family member or an acquaintance.

Once he made a visit to the Driskoll family. Mr. Driskoll was up on the housetop repairing the roof. As Kelland approached he introduced himself. After chitchatting with him, Kelland invited him and his family to church. Mr. Driskoll replied, "I don't go to church." The conversation proceeded back and forth between them until finally Mr. Driskoll said, "if you don't get out of my yard and leave me alone, I'm gonna throw this hammer at you."

With that said Kelland left but he didn't leave him out of his prayers. Two weeks later the Driskoll family came strolling under the tent, came to the altar, repented, and became devout faithful members of the church. It was a reminder to never underestimate the power of God. Praise the Lord!

We experienced many victories while getting the gospel to people of East Albany. There were the disappointments as well. Kelland learned a lot. His faith was challenged as he worked, visited, and prayed for his new congregation. But, he never gave up!

His visits took him into homes of all kinds. We had one member that was a real worker. She could visit and bring more people to Sunday School than all the rest of the church put together. Her name was Clara Lovin. Her husband was a painter (and alcoholic) but didn't attend church with her. Even though her husband was not a believer, we felt welcome in their home.

She invited us for dinner and we accepted. She was a good cook and we enjoyed her hospitality. I wanted to make myself useful by helping serve the drinks, which were iced tea and coffee. I got up from the table to serve them and asked, "Mr. Coffee, would you like some lovin?" Kelland was speechless. He was horrified at what I just said. He asked, "Nelia, do you know what you said?" Sister Lovin was laughing so hard and so was Mr. Lovin. By this time it had occurred to me what I had said. I was so embarrassed. I was apologizing and I'm sure my face totally red.

Again, Kelland followed a lead from one of the members to visit a backslidden young woman. After knocking loudly to make sure he was heard, a half-clad, barefoot woman came to the door and said, "yes, did you want to see me?" Once he saw her half naked body, he felt like rebuking her and leaving. But instead he introduced himself and invited her to church. She began pulling at her skimpy clothes trying to cover her nakedness and started to cry. He never entered the house but proceeded to talk to her about repentance through the screen door. In her confession she acknowledged being a prostitute and apologized for her appearance. She thought Kelland was a male friend who came to call on her. His call was different. He offered her repentance, new hope, and a new life as he prayed with her. Christ died for all, *Praise the Lord!*

The church grew and so did our family with the birth of Dianne in 1954. She was a ray of sunshine. I remember playing the piano with her lying across my lap to keep the mist from falling on her when it rained. We felt the wind and cold even though we had space heaters inside the tent. But, we had some wonderful church services in that tent. We came with an empty tent but left a congregation of over 140 in attendance. In a year and a half we saw the Lord add to our membership weekly. Kelland felt his work was finished and time to move on to another field of labor. We left East Albany to go back into evangelistic work as we followed the Lord's leading.

BACK ON THE EVANGELISTIC TRAIL

Once again, the Lord used our efforts mightily in revivals over the next twelve months. Kelland was booked solid. He had more churches wanting him for revival than he could get to. He was grateful to the Lord that so many needed his message for their church. He was humbled by so many invitations. We saw great numbers saved, and many healings. We rejoiced over reaping a vast harvest that year. It was more difficult evangelizing with a lively two year old. Most times we stayed in homes of the gracious pastors but occasionally had to leave Dianne with my mother because it was more convenient. Either way, it was difficult.

During the year of 1955 we were asked by State Overseer Boatwright to go to Buford Church of God, Buford, Georgia for an eight weeks period. The pastor, W.M."Doc" Horton, had suffered a heart attack and needed to be on leave from the church for rest and relaxation. We were glad and honored to help a dear friend in his time of physical distress.

The church was averaging 350-500 in Sunday School and Brother Boatwright felt Kelland would be the one to maintain the momentum of this great church. We took time from our evangelistic schedule to go as the fill-in pastor for a two-month period. It worked out great for us to gain more experience in the life of a pastor. Buford was known as a strong thriving church throughout the state and denomination. They had great leadership and we enjoyed working with them. The Wilson's, Brazwell's, and the Ramey's had large family connections in the congregation which added to their numerical and financial strength. All the names I don't remember (it's been over fifty years) but I do remember what a blessing they were to the Jeffords.

Kelland worked hard visiting day and night to keep every department of the church on an upward climb. The church was one of the most 'sought after' churches then and it is considered today one of Georgia's biggest and best.

Kelland had spoken with the State Overseer about a church to pastor since we now had a child. He did not ask for a certain size church or a certain location of one. He felt the Lord knew where we needed to be. We would keep evangelizing until that door opened. You know that is the hardest thing for the Christian is to *wait*. By nature, we human beings are so impatient. If we will *"continue to wait upon the Lord"* (Isaiah 40:31) it will come to pass.

**Nelia and Kelland
Early Ministry**

**Nelia and Kelland
1955**

Chapter 5

You Are Too Young Or Too Old

We had gone to Jesup for a visit with my parents. We went to the field to gather some green peanuts to boil. Kelland and I loved boiled peanuts...a southern delicacy. While sitting on the ground picking peanuts off the bushes, my sister, Geneva, delivered a message that State Overseer D.C. Boatwright had called wanting to get in touch with Kelland. After gathering the peanuts, we left so Kelland could see what the call was about.

He called the overseer and was told that a church had come open and he would like to appoint him as pastor. After a somewhat lengthy telephone conversation, Kelland accepted the church. In their discussion, Kelland was told when he should move there, etc. Kelland and I both were excited about the church and knew it would be challenging since it was an older settled sort of church.

State Overseer Boatwright called the Alma, Georgia church and told them who their new pastor would be. The brethren got together and called the overseer back to tell him they wanted an older more seasoned pastor. In fact, they would like to have Rev. H. M. Duck, pastor of the Palace Street Church in Griffin, Georgia. He had been pastor of the Alma church previously.

State Overseer Boatwright called Kelland back to say, "hold up, and don't start packing yet." He further explained their reasoning of wanting an older pastor. Simply put, they think you are too young. We found out, either *you are too young or too old.* I'm so thankful that the Lord does not label us as such. The Lord takes us just as we are. All he asks for is a willing heart and obedient servant. We were in God's hands and he would see that we were assigned where He wanted us. The overseer worked it out that the older pastor at Griffin, Georgia would move to the church in Alma, Georgia, thus leaving a vacancy at Griffin. Kelland was appointed pastor of Palace Street Church of God, Griffin, Georgia in September 1956, and for the next decade we marveled as God led us from victory to victory. Truly, we were in the divine will of God.

Our attendance the first Sunday was 108. The church welcomed us, but some of the congregation thought that Kelland was awfully young. One member said, "Lord help us, they have sent us a boy to pastor our church." I guess we were rather young. He was twenty-seven and I was twenty-two. Neither looked our age. But the church soon found out that the 'young boy' had a vision for the church and fire in his bones. The church would never be the same.

Kelland's eleventh commandment, "Thou shalt not do the work of ten men, but thou shalt get ten men to do the work." was thrust into action. The people loved us as we worked diligently for the church. Kelland went day and night visiting homes, hospitals, businesses, funeral homes, or wherever people could be found. Before long he would take one of the brethren with him, and another, and another. Pretty soon he had his ten men going and doing the same. The church came alive. People were getting saved. There were visitors in every service. A spirit of revival prevailed.

I organized a Ladies Trio that was soon the buzz around Griffin. They were good. People invited us to sing at homecomings, revivals, and funerals, etc. In fact, during our ten-year pastorate at Griffin, we were involved in more than five hundred funerals. Obviously, they were not all church members or their families. The three funeral homes would use us to sing, play, or preach. The uncle of the Davis Brothers restaurant chain had died and I was asked to play the organ for the funeral. When the service was over and the funeral procession was about ready to leave with several Cadillacs, Rolls-Royces and other big shinny cars in line to transport the family to the cemetery, I was stunned to see Kelland.

The funeral home staff personnel explained the minister had to leave and they had no one to do the committal at the graveside, so they called Kelland. Wherever the door of opportunity opened to us, we walked in. We reached many, many people through this means.

Every Sunday, Kelland would drive our car to pick up family after family for Sunday School. He had one large family of eight. They were dirt poor, clean in their appearance but shabbily dressed. Faithfully, Kelland would see they got to Sunday School.

One night he had a call from the hospital with the sad news that little Tommy was seriously sick and not expected to live. Kelland got there before he died. Tommy said, "I want a cowboy suit for my birthday." "Now, now, don't you worry, son you'll have the cowboy suit," replied Kelland. Little Tommy died later that night. He was buried in the cowboy suit that he asked for. Kelland was glad that he made it possible for them to be in Sunday School.

One faithful member of the church, Sister Brock, requested prayer for her family in every service. She felt a special burden for the youngest daughter and husband. He worked at the Ford Motor plant in Hapeville, Georgia. It was difficult to find the right time to visit because of his work schedule. When he was not working, he was sleeping.

One night, Clayton and Nellie were visiting her mother and Kelland stopped for a visit, too. It was obvious Clayton had been drinking. He was talking loud, using foul language, but in spite of his inebriated state, Clayton was a likable guy. He was friendly and Kelland liked him. As they engaged more into the conversation, Clayton saw a possum in the yard. He started chasing the possum down the railroad track that ran behind his mother-in-law's house. "Come on preacher help me catch the possum," Clayton called out. Kelland joined him but in their pursuit the possum got away.

Now Kelland could care less about the animal. He was interested in winning Clayton Brown to the Lord, and if it took 'chasing the possum down the railroad track', so be it. He wanted to build a relationship with Clayton and win his friendship. Maybe this could be called 'possum evangelism.' It worked! After that he liked his mother-in-law's preacher.

Kelland suspected one of the older ladies was dipping snuff. He surprised her one day with a visit. It was obvious she had snuff in her lower lip. He asked, "Granny, do you have a dip of snuff in your mouth?" "Well," she said, "Bro. Jeffords, I have so much vict'ry that I have to dip a little snuff to quench the spirit." He laughed so at her answer and was still laughing the day we left Griffin.

While walking down the hospital corridor, Kelland heard a man in distress calling for help. He entered the room and introduced himself, asking if he could help. Would you like for me to pray for you? The man replied, "No, no, no, get me a doctor and you can pray later." He went for the doctor and before he got back to the room the man had died.

For years each Thursday night was visitation night at the church. The Sunday School absentees were visited, plus others. Kelland would visit with the men, and I would visit with the ladies. I had got back home before the men returned. The telephone rang asking for Brother Jeffords to come quickly as Clayton and Nellie were there under conviction and needed prayer. I told Sister Brock that he had not returned from visitation but I would ask Irene Lynch and Bernice Dunn, two powerful prayer warriors of the church, to go immediately. By the time Kelland got to Sis Brock's house, he found them praising God and rejoicing. It was an answer to prayer to see this young couple come to the Lord.

They became true servants of the Lord. The next year was a time of spiritual growth for them. Clayton worked in any capacity where needed. The church couldn't afford to hire a music director so he became the choir director. His enthusiasm made up for lack of musical training and the choir was filled to overflowing.

One Sunday night while the choir was singing, the power fell with people shouting and praising the Lord. Not knowing a stray cat had gotten into the church baptistery, the loud singing excited the cat. That scared cat came leaping through the baptistery window so fast, through where the choir members stood, and high-tailed it out of there. It happened so quickly the congregation could only see the choirs' response. Choir members were bumping into each other, jumping out of the way; it was pandemonium! The congregation wasn't aware of the cat but only the sudden reaction of the choir to what had just happened. They thought the choir was experiencing an outpouring of the Holy Spirit, so they joined in and acted accordingly.

In 1959, we had the dedication of our new church building. We outgrew the old sanctuary and a larger one was needed to accommodate the growing congregation. On that November day of dedication it was filled to capacity. Additional property was purchased next to the church for expansion. Oh, how the Lord blessed! *"God is Faithful,* by whom ye were called unto the fellowship of His Son Jesus Christ Our Lord" 1 Corinthians 1:9.

Our family grew as the church grew. In 1959, Kelland Keith, Jr. and in 1963, Danita Kay joined our family. We were now a family of five. Dianne was such a blessing to us when our organist moved away. At age nine, she started playing the organ for the church. She was extremely talented, which was a gift from the Lord. Her singing, as well as her playing, blessed all who heard her.

Numerical and spiritual growths were seen in all departments of the church, but none more than the youth department. It exploded and we were thankful for that. *Young people are the energy of the church.* If you have an active group of teens that love the Lord, you will have a church that's alive and doing well. Their *enthusiastic spirit* is contagious.

On Friday night, the young people met for prayer upstairs in the corner room of the educational building. They referred to it as *"the upper room."* At that time, we had over one hundred youth that were filled with the Holy Ghost. They actively involved in every phase of church work. At visitation they were there. At revivals they were there. At a church workday they were there. Anything that was going on these young people could be counted on.

The big Sunday School push was in the Spring Enlargement Campaign. Each year it was a great event. It was launched with an enormous media campaign. It seemed the whole city knew we were in this vast outreach and the response was massive. In ten years the attendance went from 108 to 1,326 on Easter Sunday. And, this was the day before *Mega Churches and Walmart Supercenters.*

Kelland gained rapport with the textile mill superintendents. There were eighteen of them in the city. Griffin was a cotton mill town. Before the big day, he would visit the mills on all three shifts inviting people to attend church on Easter Sunday. He just wanted people to be in church. If not Palace Street, go to 'a church'. The mill superintendents liked his approach because dedicated church employees made better workers.

Many churches across the nation followed his example and started a drive each spring to boost their attendance on Easter. Space prevents me recalling all the wonderful experiences we experienced at Palace Street Church. The people were a dedicated, loving, and committed group that loved the Lord. We never forgot them. I guess you could say, "it was our first love as a pastor."

Clayton and Nellie Brown felt the call to full-time ministry. They had worked faithfully in whatever capacity needed in the Palace Street church. They had served the church with gladness and with enthusiasm. Kelland set him forth in ministry and recommend him for his first church. He knew Clayton would do well as he gave all to the work of the Lord. We missed them but wished them God's speed.

A group of members from the E. Fourth Street Church of God in Dayton, Ohio had heard about the fiery pastor of Griffin. The church was loosing its pastor and they came to see if Kelland would accept the church in Dayton. He served ten successful and wonderful years as pastor at Griffin. Kelland's vision to build a new and larger church came to fruition. We saw an explosion of growth in attendance and finance. Gaining respect and honor among businesses in the city; he was voted runner-up for 'Man of the Year'.

Maybe it was time to move on, but in his mind, he would never be more loved than in Griffin, Georgia. It wasn't easy leaving Georgia where we had spent the most of our ministry. He was loved and respected among the Church of God membership of his beloved state. He had served on every state board namely: State Council, State Youth and Christian Education Board, State Evangelism Board, State Trustee, and on appointed boards and committees.

His willingness to serve wherever needed was commendable, even if it meant moving to another state.   I knew Kelland would be successful wherever he served. He had a strong *faith* in God, and he had faith in himself.   He had a heart for the work of God and unwavering belief that *"all things are possible with God"*.

A song that became our signature song and perhaps the most requested one that we sang was, *"Til The Storm Passes By"*. The lyrics are quite meaningful and comforting. Little did I know that this song would sustain me and my faith in the months and years to come. I found out through every trial, regardless how severe, if we will just remain steadfast with our trust in Him, he will keep us safe "til' the storm passes by".

How many times has Satan told you and me there's no end of sorrow? There's no hope. There's no need to try. Just give up. But the long night that seems endless will end and the storms will comes no more. He will stand with us and keep us til' the storm passes by. Watching the storm clouds gather and listening to the thunder roll in the natural can be quite frightening. But, we know He is with us and no matter how severe the storms clouds may become, He will keep us safe til' we reach the other shore.

The song's author, Mosie Lister, was truly inspired the day he penned these words. Through the years they have given courage to the discouraged and hope to the hopeless. May many more be blessed by its message.

Griffin Church of God - 216 Palace Street - Griffin, Georgia

New Palace Street Church - Griffin, GA

Dianne, Nelia & Kelland
1955

Kelland, Nelia, Dianne, Keith
1960

Danita, Nelia, Dianne, Keith and Kelland
Christmas, 1964

**Kelland Jeffords
Griffin, GA.**

Kelland - Birthday Celebration

Nelia - Danita - Kelland
Dianne - Keith
Anniversity Sunday @ Griffin, GA

The Kelland Jeffords Family
1964

Dedication of New Sanctuary-Griffin, Ga.
Pastor Kelland Jeffords – State Overseer W. E. Johnson
October 1963

Sunday School Elected Officials
Cliff Collins, Pastor Jeffords, Alvin Gardner, Jack Kidd, Roy Goens
Griffin, Georgia

Pastor Jeffords & Clayton Brown
Griffin, Georgia

Pastor Kelland Jeffords with Church Council
Griffin, Georgia

Pastor Appreciation Day – 1960
Griffin Church of God
Griffin, Georgia

a half years ago was 129 and last Easter Sunday you were second in attendance in the city with 949 in Sunday School. This church has a monthly attendance average of over 500 in Sunday School. The Church property value of $55,000 in 1956 has been increased to over $145,000 with the purchase of more property within the next few days.

"Rev. Jeffords, we appreciate men and talent such as yours and we are glad to have you in our city to make it a better place to live."

Ed Crawford, Spalding Juvenile Probation officer, said:

"We appreciate your work and efforts. I have worked with you on various occasions and it has been a pleasure. I see when you came to Griffin you had eight young people in your church. Today you have 149 enrolled in the Youth Department. Keep up the good work, because work such as this keeps me from having a job, and I like it that way."

MEMORABLE TRIBUTES FROM FAMILY AND FRIENDS

Dear Nelia,

My recollections of life in the Jeffords home are somewhat scattered. After all, it was 41 years ago, the summer of 1965, between my freshman and sophomore years at Lee College. Kelland Jeffords was glad to open his home and churh to Lee students who needed a place to land, and a place to work for the summer. I was one of the first, followed by Dawn Wooderson and Sandy Hitte. I taught piano lessons to students in the church and generally participated in the life of the church and the Jeffords home.

My pervasive memory of Kelland Jeffords is of a man who had a great sense of humor and found the funny side of most situations. He also loved to eat, and Nelia was a wonderful cook. How could I forget *tostados?* They became a staple in my home, and after introducing them to the larger Conn family, they became a family favorite in their home as well.   Then there was all the Southern fried okra and coconut cake, made from scratch. I gained about 15 pounds that summer, and had to buy some new clothes before camp meeting because I couldn't fit into the ones in my closet.

I'll never forget going water skiing with the family, back when "mixed bathing".was a definite no-no! If I remember correctly, Kelland had never skied before, and was unable to stand up on the skis, so squatted on the skis as we zoomed along, bouncing up and down and hitting the water repeatedly with his backside. The rest of us nearly fell out of the boat laughing as he battled to stay on his feet.

As I've observed people over the years, I've come to feel that Kelland Jeffords had a quality that is perhaps one of the most important. I don't remember him for his sermons in church. I do remember him because he believed in helping young people by giving them an opportunity and then encouraging them; and I do mean *young* people (I was 19 the summer that I spent in Griffin, GA). I picked up bits of wisdom for life, not in formal, intentional ways, but sitting at the dining room table, thrown in midst jokes and anecdotes of his days at Lee and his years in the ministry. He also invited my husband, Paul, a college senior at that time to come and hold a revival in his church in Dayton, Ohio the summer before we were married. Paul remembers the same sense of fun and learning by going along with Kelland on his pastoral rounds. Kelland was a born mentor before the word or concept came into vogue.

This impact on younger people was never more evident than at Kelland's funeral, which was one of the longest I had been to at the time, and filled with people I'd never met who talked about his caring influence on their various lives.

Love,

Darlia

Darlia McLuhan Conn

Kelland Jeffords

I am Rodney Jeffords, first cousin of Kelland Jeffords, and I would like to share with you what his life and ministry meant to me.

Growing up in the town of Waresboro, Georgia, as a lad I remember Kelland as a young man called to minister. When he would make visits to Waresboro, he always had time to talk with me and find out my plans for the future. His Christian life and testimony had a lasting influence on my life.

One of my fondest memories took place in the summer between my junior and senior year in high school. During this time, I had the opportunity to spend several weeks in Griffin, Georgia with Kelland, his family, and Church. The Griffin Church had experienced tremendous growth under Kelland's leadership and I had the privilege to learn from him what it would take to be a successful Pastor. Also, during this time as a young teenage evangelist, he allowed me to preach in his great Church. He was also instrumental in helping me secure other ministry opportunities. I will never forget the interest he had in my ministry. He was helpful in so many ways, taking time to listen to me; teaching me; allowing me to do hands on ministry with him; showing me the true heart of a Pastor. Before the Church understood the mentoring process, Kelland Jeffords, understood the process and was willing to invest in hundred's of young men and women including myself.

To you who have, or may in the future, receive assistance from the Lee University/Kelland Jeffords Scholarship Fund, let me list some qualities of his life and some things I learned from him:

1. *He was a man of the people.*
He was a man who built relationships with people. He lived among the people of his church and city. He reached out to everyone regardless of age, educational background or social status. It can truly be said of him "That he never met a stranger."
2. *He had a special place in his heart for young people.*

Every Church he pastored had a very active youth group. When I visited his Church in Griffin, Georgia in the 1960"s, his youth group was more than one hundred in attendance. As a young Minister, he always worked in State Youth Camps. He also served as Youth and Christian Education Director for the Church of God in the state of Georgia. Thousands of young people were influenced to love and serve God through the life and ministry of Kelland Jeffords.

3. *He loved and supported Lee University.*
Kelland wanted the Youth of his day to receive a Christian education. Therefore, he challenged and encouraged hundreds of Teens to attend Lee University. Not only did he encourage them, he became personally involved in helping them fulfill their dream to attend a great Bible-based university.

4. *He was a great soul-winner.*
Being a Pastor of the people, he won many souls to the Lord by witnessing to them in homes, hospitals, jails, restaurants and businesses. Every ministry activity he was involved in was motivated by his desire to win the lost.

5. *He was a man of the Spirit.*
He truly believed in spirit-led worship. He often declared that it is "not by might nor by power but by my spirit saith the Lord of Host." In every facet of his ministry, he relied on the unction and power of the Holy Spirit to accomplish great things for God.

The legacy of Kelland Jeffords is still in the hearts and souls of those who knew and loved him. Still today, nineteen years after his passing, every time I think of Kelland Jeffords, a smile comes to my face.

Rodney Jeffords
Administrative Bishop, Church of God in Pennsylvania

MEMORIES OF A FRIENDSHIP BETWEEN TWO MINISTERS OF DIFFERENT RELIGIOUS ORGANIZATIONS

By

E. P. Pruett

We met as pastors in Griffin, Georgia around 1960. Kelland was pastor of the Palace Street Church of God and I was pastor of First Assembly of God.

In those days, the church was judged by the size of Sunday School attendance and Kelland was a Sunday School builder. Actually, I worked hard for numbers, too. Our two churches were near the same in number of Sunday School attendees. To the best of my recollection, at that time our Sunday Schools were in the 400 – 600 brackets. The two of us had a friendly rivalry.

Kelland was a good pastor. He loved people and was what I call *a people pastor.* Personally, I felt as a pastor, I needed a real close friend with whom I could, when necessary, "let my hair down". Ministers go through very stressful times and need someone with whom they can confide in and live life, not just as a preacher, but as a normal human being. Kelland was what I called a real "tonic" for me. He was full of life, humorous, and a real pleasure to be around. We became the dearest of friends and spent lots of time together.

Not only did he have one of the larger churches in Griffin but very well known in his religious organization, *Church of God,* and was respected as one of their leaders throughout the state and nation. Both he and I had a daily radio ministry for years which brought us together in many situations since we were pastors in the same city. We became involved in business ownership together. I can say without a doubt that he was one of the best business partners that I ever had. We became owners of the Griffin Hotel in downtown Griffin. He was one of the original stockholders in Brightmoor Nursing Home in Griffin. We, also, owned a motel and restaurant in

Eufaula, Alabama, plus, other ventures.   All were successful businesses and it was a pleasure having him as a partner.

We enjoyed many trips together.   Some that come to mind was the Church of God General Assembly in Dallas, Texas.   Another time I was going to a meeting at the Assemblies of God General Headquarters in Springfield, Missouri.   I drove the Jeffords car for them as far as St. Louis as they were going to their General Assembly.   Kelland had a carbuncle on the back of his neck that grew worse on the way.   By the time we arrived in St. Louis, he had to be hospitalized.   Unfortunately, he was not able to attend the conference at all.   He was a faithful Church of God minister and was counted as one of the most loyal to his Fellowship.

Then, there was the New York City incident.   Kelland and Nelia were vacationing with her sister across the river in New Jersey. They drove into the city and met me at JFK Airport.   We attended the New York World's Fair together, which was an awesome experience.   We went to a restaurant, saw the Rocketts at Radio City Music Hall, and took in a very good clean movie.   This was an enjoyable time in our lives together.   Note: The year slips my mind. After all, I'm 86 years young.

I met Kelland's wonderful parents while taking one of our trips. They were business people in the small South Georgia town. Kelland's father owned and operated a successful grocery store (Jeffords Grocery), and his mother was the 'Postmaster' in Waresboro, Georgia.   They were outstanding citizens of that area.

Also, I met Nelia's family in Jesup, Georgia.   I found the Flowers Family to be prominent citizens of that area.   It was a pleasure to meet both families and enjoy their Christian fellowship.

Nelia Jeffords was an excellent musician and choir director.   She won many honors while directing them.   Her group won National Teen Talent twice as the best choir in the nation.   She took the choir on tour to England to minister in song and represent the Church of God.   They were a select band of young people whose talent gained recognition throughout the denomination.

Kelland and Nelia had great aspirations for their three children: Dianne, Keith, and Danita. They have become very successful in their chosen career fields. Keith became a prominent Plastic Surgeon and he has, in fact, cut on me a bit!

Because ministers go in different geographical directions, some of my last physical connections with Kelland were when he pastored the Rainbow Church of God in Decatur, Georgia. This was in the 1980's. I was planning on moving to Tampa, Florida. At this time, Kelland's health was a serious problem. His diabetic condition had affected his eyes and he needed my help with the church. When I talked with the Jeffords, I asked them if they felt that the Lord was not through with them at the church; if the Lord would have them to stay on as pastors. They assured me that God was not through with them yet and felt I should come help them. However, my plans to go to Tampa were put on hold. I went on the church staff and worked with them for about six months. God blessed our efforts together and the Jeffords had a good ministry there. I remember visiting and preaching for them when they pastored in Ohio. I was privileged to work with them for a short while during his pastorate in Mableton, Georgia. Our paths crossed over the years and it was always a joy for both of us. Our friendship remains until this day.

Most of us go our separate ways in life. After some years following Kelland's death, Nelia remarried and continues in ministry and the work of the Lord. The family is blessed and will be remembered as outstanding members in the Body of Christ.

I can say my life is far richer in many ways because of Kelland K. Jeffords and his wonderful family. In spite of my advanced age, I'm still active in the work of the Lord. At present, I'm on staff at Evangel Temple in Morrow, Georgia (the Atlanta area).

At Kelland's memorial service, I believe there were thirteen speakers and it was my honor to be the first one. Many things come and go, but precious memories last forever.

Much love to the Kelland K. Jeffords family. We'll meet you in Heaven.

Ernest P. Pruett
1603 Rosewood Drive
Griffin, Georgia 30223

ONE OF A KIND

The Rev. Kelland K. Jeffords was one 'special' guy. He was witty, humorous, sharp as a tack, and filled with wisdom. These attributes, linked with a genuine dedication to God and a sincere commitment to ministry, made him one of our finest pastors.

I first met Brother Kelland when he was pastor of Palace Street Church of God in Griffin, Georgia. It was Homecoming Day. He had invited my family and me to be the special singers and speaker for the occasion. What a day it was! There were people everywhere. Pastor Jeffords had them all excited and we just about had to run all day to keep up with his program. I well remember how impressed I was with the passion and enthusiasm the pastor showed in dealing with, and leading his church. That day he became one of my greatly admired friends for life.

Through the years we have worked together in several capacities. He served with me as the State Youth and Christian Education Director of Georgia when I was General Youth and Christian Education Director. He served as pastor of the Mableton Church of God while I was State Overseer of North Georgia. Whatever he did, he did it well. In fact, every church where he served as pastor experienced substantial growth while he was there.

He had a 'special' wife, Nelia. She was a great worker. She was spiritual and knew how to pray, which probably accounted for much of the spiritual growth of his churches. She was a wonderful musician and in each service anchored the music portion at the piano. She was a great choir director and especially loved to work with young people. They always had a championship youth choir.

He and Nelia had two beautiful daughters and a handsome, brilliant son. They were always a credit to their parents.

Something else really special about Kelland was his wit. Once he went to see Brother H.B.Ramsey when Bro. Ramsey served as overseer of North Georgia about a little problem he was dealing with. Bro. Ramsey was seated behind his desk. Kelland was seated in a chair across the desk in front of him. It was just after lunch and while Kelland expounded the problem he noticed that Bro. Ramsey had fallen asleep. He knew that Bro. Ramsey had been working hard and he didn't want to wake him, so he pulled his chair up close to the desk, lays his head over on the desk and went to sleep, too. Bro. Ramsey awoke with a snore and snort, which nearly scared Kelland to death. Bro. Ramsey clapped his hands and said: "Bro. Kelland, let's urn-urn-get an ice cream cone." It has been one of my favorite stories for years.

Another time, the North Georgia State Council was meeting at Lake Lanier in a hotel. Dr. Paul Walker had come into my room and we were chatting. Other members kept coming by the room and soon the room was filled. For more than an hour, Kelland entertained us by telling humorous happenings in his life and ministry. He kept us in sidesplitting laughter, and not a story was made up.

He was greatly respected in the area where he served as a fine quality pastor and a progressive leader.

We were good friends for many years. His children Dianne, Keith and Danita were my buddies. I performed the wedding ceremony for Danita and her fiancé, Bob. When Kelland passed away, Nelia asked me to speak at his funeral. When I arrived at the Rainbow Drive Church of God in Decatur, Georgia, I learned I was the seventeenth speaker on the program. See what I mean about him being *special?* What funeral can you remember speaking at who had sixteen other speakers? He was 'one of a kind'. His influence still affects many.

His family set up an endowment at Lee University to provide *scholarship funds* for worthy students. It would be wonderful if every student receiving help from this fund could be given a copy of this book so they could see what kind of "A Special Person" this was that is helping them.

PAUL F HENSON, Retired
Friend of Kelland Jeffords

MEMORIES OF MY FRIEND, KELLAND K. JEFFORDS, SR.

It was 1954 when I met the Jeffords that then consisted of Kelland, Nelia and little Dianne. They had begun the East Albany Church earlier and were then a very talented Evangelism Team. It seemed that our families became friends almost immediately.

In the beginning of my remarks, let me state that this couple was a team. They complimented each other to the fullest.

The move that was to identify Kelland Jeffords came in 1956 when he was assigned the pastorate at Palace Street Church in Griffin, Georgia. For the next decade, this young couple helped light up the city for God. It was there that Keith and Danita joined the team. Kelland Jeffords and Griffin, Georgia became synonymous terms.

Kelland also left his ministerial marks on other churches including Dayton, Ohio, Atlanta-Southside, Mableton, and Rainbow Drive, Decatur.

If you wonder what made Kelland's ministry so effective, it was the fact that he had certain principles that made accomplishment and progress *a natural thing*. Not only did those principles make for effective ministry, but they spilled over to his children. They all three have excelled in their respective fields. And, to the young ministers who came under his leadership which includes Clayton Brown, Steve Land, Jim Bolin, Edgar Waters, Tim Trotter, David Gibson to name a few.

He was a lively spirit- *unique* – humorous-committed-gifted- but most of all he was fully alive- *alive for Jesus Christ!*

He was a *communicator* in his own inhibited way. His stories, the relation of humorous happenings - often graphic – were laced into his sermons and will be told and retold again and again for years to come. His ministry was very effective in drawing people to the Lord.

He was *people centered*. The young, the old, and all ages in between knew that he was their friend. He was a master at human relationships. His big secrets were *care and love!*

He was *loyal*. His Church of God roots go back to his childhood when noted ministers, General Overseers and State Overseers, would visit in his parent's home in Waresboro, Georgia. He had a very deep love for his parents, Clyde and Isabel Jeffords, his brother Raymond, and his sister Marilyn. He was a loyal husband, father, and friend. This was so obviously demonstrated at the funeral when the church at Rainbow Drive in Decatur, Ga. was filled to overflowing.

Kelland and I were business partners in an endeavor over a number of years. The location of business was in Eufaula, Alabama. Our occasional trips there were memorable. We would share and confide as trusting friends. Incidentally, we never had one business misunderstanding. He was a good associate.

We would usually stop along the way from Atlanta to Eufaula at some small town restaurant or at a country store for a coke and crackers. He never met a stranger. I would always be amazed at the way people would share with him and talk as if he were their friend.

His health deteriorated rapidly in his latter years. Yet, he continued to minister to his church at Rainbow Drive, in Decatur, Ga. until the very end of his life. He never realized that he gave the ultimate sacrifice. This never crossed his mind. His enthusiastic spirit transcended his infirmities.

What a great friend he was to me and to thousands more.

Clarence Busby Sr

Clarence Busby Sr., State Secretary
Churches of God in Georgia (1954-1974)

KELLAND K. JEFFORDS
by CLARENCE BUSBY, JR.

When I read the letter that dad wrote about his good friend Kelland Jeffords, I was reminded of not just how good of friends they were, but how they were truly "buddies". Clarence Busby, Sr. had two sibling brothers, but not one of them as close as Brother Kelland. I doubt that in the thirty-three years they knew each other there were few weeks that went by that they didn't have some conversation either by phone or meeting at some restaurant like the Waffle House or McDonalds for a cup of coffee and a "little chat." Sometimes they talked about taking a trip together, other times about some business dealings, but more often than not, it was about how much they loved the great Church of God: How if they were in charge, this is how they would handle things.

They had something else in common. They loved ministry and they loved fellow ministers. Some people like to talk about other people and sometimes in not too flattery of a way but Kelland and dad talked about ministers. With great admiration and tremendous respect, they discussed and 'spoke prophecies' of the next great young minister to show himself in Georgia. It was like the "battle of the bands", but it was the "battle of the preachers". Who was the greatest preacher in the church? Church of God, that is. *I'm not sure that they knew there were any others.* Was it Ray Hughes, Paul H. Henson, Paul L Walker or some other most admired? Who would be the next General Overseer? They knew their "stuff", their church stuff. And they loved their ministry friends. They swapped stories, told their tales about "their" church and "their ministry friends."

Over the years there are times that you need someone special, not just anyone, but a *special* friend that no matter what would be there to share the pains of this life. Kelland Jeffords was that man for my dad. He knew that he could tell Kelland anything, even secret things, and Kelland would be there, standing side by side, with a hand on his shoulder and a tear running down his cheek, he would be there. A "sticketh closer than a brother" friend. One who knew you on the good days and would stay there with you on the bad days. A "no matter what" friend.   A man who would pray for you and expect God to answer and answer real quick Lord for this is my friend. They truly were the "best of buddies".

Honoring Clyde Jeffords for 44 yrs.
As church clerk
Pastor W.F. Spivey and Kelland Jeffords

Kelland was a great friend and mentor

When I think of Kelland, I am flooded with nostalgic feelings of warmth, acceptance, friendship, and example. I think of his wonderful spirit of excitement and enthusiasm for life and for ministry. His drive and indomitable spirit to build the kingdom of God on earth through the church made an indelible mark on my life and ministry.

Kelland was a great friend and mentor to me in the early formative years of my ministry. Many of the things that influenced my style of pastoral ministry I learned while serving for a short time as youth pastor under his tutelage and direction. It was an exciting time for me to observe and to learn from this man, whom I considered a master pastor. His success was, I felt, due to God's evident calling upon his life and his great love and enthusiasm for that call. He applied himself and his many talents and giftings unreservedly in bringing honor to God and his family. I was blessed to be influenced by serving with him.

Kelland was always affable, approachable, and affirming. I felt welcome in the home of Kelland and Nelia, which was always good for a laugh, a hug, and a word of encouragement. I always felt accepted and they never gave me the feeling I was intruding or was a nuisance, though, looking back, I'm sure I was. They were definitely graced with the gift of hospitality. Thank you, Kelland and Nelia, for being so gracious and good to me. I was lonely and in need of encouragement and you were there. I am deeply indebted to you both.

In working with Kelland, I observed his genuine love and concern for his flock. Always caring, he made himself available to the people. When visiting in their homes, I noted his tenderness toward them and the short but always shepherding prayer for their situation to improve. His church grew because people knew he really cared. I learned to be effective in visitation is to be lovingly focused on the reason for the visit, talk briefly, pray briefly and leave.

When I was Kelland's youth pastor, we all went to visit our folks in South Georgia for the Christmas holidays. We were to meet back on Friday to get ready for the Sunday services. We arrived back in Griffin, Georgia, where Kelland and Nelia pastored a great church, which had exploded in growth under their dynamic leadership. It was about 7:00 p.m. on a very cold, late December Friday evening. Immediately, Kelland exclaimed, "Come on, Robert, let's go make some visits for Sunday." His energy was seemingly inexhaustible.

Kelland's work habits were enviable. Never lazy, but always energetic toward God's work, he was blessed by God to accomplish so much with a life that was taken from us way too soon. He used what he had to maximum potential.

Kelland and Nelia were a team, truly one in the call of God upon their lives. And what a team they were! Their creative skills were to be envied. They worked hard and were rewarded with excellence for their commitment. Whether in Sunday School promotion, revival, or Teen Talent, they were highly successful in their pursuit of excellence for God and His church.

Kelland was also conscious of the finances of the church. Counting the cost and being careful not to over commit and burden the people with more than they could adequately handle. He could squeeze all the benefit from a dollar whether it was the church's or his own. He was careful with the money people sacrificed and gave.

Kelland's organizational skills were, I feel, ahead of his time. Along with the organizational insight was the ability to involve others in ministry, utilizing the various talents God had placed in the church. To be able to organize and to place people in the area of their giftings is to be admired. Not only did Kelland excel in these areas, but then he motivated these people to accomplish what they were expected to do.

Others recognize leaders for their success in what they accomplish. Kelland was a leader. To those who were blessed to grow personally along with the growth of the churches he pastored, to those who called him friend, to those who sat in classes he taught, to those who called him family, we were blessed to have shared in his life.

Not only did Kelland excel in God's call on his life, but instilled in his children a drive for excellence in their lives. You kids have done that and have done your dad and mom proud. I too applaud you. The fruit is good.

Finally, the best word to describe Kelland is the sometimes overused and misused word: unique. He was truly one of a kind in the truest and best sense of the word. I am so thankful for your influence on my life and ministry. I miss you, old friend.

Robert P. Herrin Sr. Pastor
Plant City Church of God
Plant City Florida

CEDAR VALLEY CATHEDRAL OF PRAISE

2744 CLEVELAND HIGHWAY – DALTON, GEORGIA

CLAYTON BROWN, SENIOR PASTOR

I can remember well the first time I met and got acquainted with Kelland Jeffords. My mother-in-law was a member of his church, Palace Street Church of God. My wife and I were not Christians and not churchgoers.

It was a church night (Wednesday I think) and my mother-in-law had gone to church. Pastor Jeffords brought her home. My wife, Nellie, and I happened to be there. About the time he drove up to Nanny Brock's house a 'possum' ran across the road. He jumped out of the car, and a chase pursued after the animal. He yelled, "let's get him" and away we ran down the railroad track behind my mother-in-law's house.

He was dressed in a suit because he had just come from church. I was in casual clothes and appropriately attired for the chase. We ran after the 'possum' but he got away. One thing was accomplished though….I got acquainted with 'Nanny Brock's pastor. And, I thought to myself, "now, that's my kind of man".

Nellie and I were again visiting at Nanny Brock's house on a Thursday night. The Lord had been dealing with me and I was under ole' time conviction. Nanny recognized our condition and knew what we needed is prayer. She called the pastor's home for him to come but he was not home yet from visitation. Instead, Sister Jeffords sent two ladies and told Nanny that she would send Pastor as soon as he came in.

Irene Lynch and Bernice Dunn came right away and began praying with my wife and me. Pastor Jeffords came shortly afterwards and found us praising God and rejoicing because we had repented and shouts of victory rang throughout the house. We had a great time of rejoicing! Can you imagine what the angels in heaven were doing because a sinner had come home?

I came to church still praising with shouts of joy. My sins were forgiven and I wanted all that God had for me. Later, I joined the church and Brother Jeffords became my pastor. *He is the only pastor I ever had.*

I was pliable and wanted to work in the church. I was willing to do anything. Pastor Jeffords and Nelia got me involved by involving me with various programs in the church. First, working with a small boys class (I have four daughters). Then, with visitation teams that went out every Thursday night visiting the sick, new prospects, and Sunday School absentees. And, it wasn't long I was singing in the choir. The church didn't have a music director so what did I do – began leading the choir.

For all the success I have had in advancing kingdom work here at Cedar Valley Cathedral of Praise in Dalton, Georgia, I learned from Brother Jeffords at the Palace Street Church of God in Griffin, Georgia. All the wisdom and understanding came from him in caring for my church. Pastor Jeffords became my *mentor.*

Kelland Jeffords is still 'my pastor.' I'm looking forward to seeing him again. We will talk and reminisce about the good times; the wonderful services and fellowships we enjoyed at Palace Street Church. It will be a grand reunion!

I saw in my Pastor a real example of a caring pastor that loved, nurtured, and taught them the way of salvation. And that I have tried to follow.

CLAYTON BROWN, SENIOR PASTOR
CEDAR VALLEY CATHEDRAL OF PRAISE

Chapter 6

The Move North That Didn't Last Long

Kelland accepted the pastorate in Dayton, and what a challenge this turned out to be. The church was divided into three groups and this is the way they sat in church. Their former pastor had a serious personal problem and this was the result. He immediately saw what would be his mission.

He concentrated on getting the church unified, and members paying their tithes to pay unpaid bills. The first men's meeting had almost turned into a fistfight as tempers flared. Men pointing their finger in each other's face, making threats to each other. At the altar while lifting their hands in prayer would have their arms jerked down by those in disagreement. All members were committed to the church but allowed Satan to bring division amongst the brethren. It was carnality at the highest level.

My sister and brother-in-law, Aletha and Edgar Waters, from Jesup, Georgia, came on staff and worked as the assistant pastor. They were just starting in the ministry and this was their first assignment. He and Kelland labored together diligently to move the church forward. We will always be indebted to them for their excellent assistantship in ministry while in Dayton.

For the next thirteen months we would pray, use all the godly wisdom at our discretion, and great revivals to bring the church into unity. That is exactly what happened. We saw the church reunited and working together. We set new Sunday School attendance and tithe records. Kelland felt he had accomplished what God intended for him to do.

At a called meeting of the men he resigned as pastor. Every man stood up and pleaded with him to stay and pledged their support. He told them of his appreciation but said he felt this was God's will for him to leave.

East Fourth Street Church of God
Dayton, Ohio

Kelland and Nelia
Dayton, Ohio

MEMORABLE TRIBUTES FROM, FAMILY AND FRIENDS

"UNIQUE, SPECIAL, ONE OF A KIND"

by

Reverend J. Edgar Waters

Unique, special, one of a kind" are definitely words to describe my friend and brother in-law, Kelland Jeffords. His uniqueness was apparent even in his sermons. His illustrations were well remembered, perhaps because of his use of a special *gift of humor,* and because they sprang from the most ordinary happenings of life. He might describe a bird or a squirrel, but by the time he finished talking about it, it would be the most unusual bird or squirrel one had ever heard of and serve as a profound object lesson.

Kelland was, also, well known for his *gift of enthusiasm and encouragement.* He mentored many people as they worked with him at his various pastorates. It has been said the working with Kelland could earn one equivalent of a "pastoral degree". He knew how to encourage and direct young ministers and he certainly did that for me.

He had an acute awareness of the moving of the Holy Spirit. In the spring of 1966 he and Nelia had been seeking God for someone to assist them at the Palace Street Church of God in Griffm, Georgia. They stated that every time they prayed, Aletha and I would come up before them. Even though they knew I had a good job and had no need to leave it, they obeyed the leading of the Lord. They came to our home unexpectedly to tell us, not knowing that two days before, I had paced an ad in the local paper to liquidate our assets in order to answer God's call. None of our family knew that God had been dealing with me, as we had told no one at that time. Such was Kelland's dependence upon the moving of the Spirit. We agreed to pray about a move to Griffin in September. Kelland advised us to just trust the Lord and be ready to do His will.

In August, while attending the General Assembly, Kelland accepted an appointment as pastor of the East Fourth Street Church of God in

Dayton, Ohio. We helped them move. Kelland was a most wise administrator and instinctively knew how to work with people. At his first Pastor's Council meeting, he discussed his need for someone to assist him in his work. Stating that "though the Waters family did not come with him as a package deal," he would appreciate them considering me along with any others they might have in mind to work with him. He further explained that if they did choose me, I would not be coming as a preacher but as someone to work with music, office, and visitation. The church previously had three staff members working in those areas. I was hired and during that year I received my ministerial license.

This began for me some of the greatest training a person could have. Kelland Jeffords was an absolute genius as a pastor. And, this was most evident in visitation. He taught me how to make a hospital visit; what kind of evangelists to use for specific needs of the church, and how to deal with problems that most likely would arise. He knew people, loved people and knew how to talk to them. As I followed him day by day, I saw what pastoring and mentoring was all about. I witnessed a level of integrity which was above reproach. He truly was an honorable man and a great gentleman; also, a very funny one.

Everybody that knew Kelland was aware how he loved Georgia and the Atlanta area. One day he told me, "Edgar, I am going back to Georgia. You need to book some revivals". After about thirteen months as pastor of the East Fourth Street Church he resigned. He accepted the pastorate of the Southside Church of God in Atlanta. I was called to pastor the Waresboro, Georgia Church of God the summer of 1967. In February of 1969 I was elected pastor of the East Point Church of God where I retired in 2004 after serving the church for thirty-five years.

In 1970 Kelland became State Youth and Christian Education Director of Georgia. This was a great forum to showcase his and Nelia's love of youth; unusual administrative and programming abilities. Aletha and I were privileged to work with them in youth camps and wherever needed. In every situation Kelland was there when I needed him and always willing to share his insights with me. Reflecting on the memories of those days has brought many chuckles and lots of joyful remembrances.

It was so sad to see Kelland go from being a healthy, energetic man I had known in earlier years, to his final days as diabetes took its toll. As we sat with the family at the hospital those last days, we all prayed and committed him into God's hands. We know our loss was Heaven's gain but it was a great loss to the church. Such pastors and leaders do not happen very often.

I was privileged and honored to help with his funeral. The outpouring of love from his many, many friends and fellow ministers was beautiful to behold. It was as if we were all wrapped in the love of God as we mourned the loss of our loved one and experience such a spirit of worship and celebration.

Reflecting on these treasured memories I have been reminded of those powerful words that ring with such authority, "Be Thou Faithful Unto Death, And I Will Give Thee A Crown Of Life."

Reverend J. Edgar Waters
Retired Church of God Minister

Chapter 7

Moves Back To Georgia

Kelland loved his home state of Georgia. He made the statement: "If I'm gonna fight the devil, then I will fight him on my home turf." He was happy to be on his way back to the place he loved. When we crossed the Georgia state line he stopped the car, got out, knelt down, and kissed the ground. We all burst out laughing and couldn't believe he was actually kissing the ground. We were all convinced he was glad to be back in Georgia.

We left a church with an attendance of eight hundred and took a church in Atlanta, Ga. that had eighty-eight the first Sunday. What a psychological experience! But, it wouldn't stay that way for long.

Our pastorate at the Southside Church would span three and one half years of growth in every department: Sunday School, Tithes, Youth, Membership, etc. We went through remodeling of the church and paving the parking lot.

Kelland's *love* and *compassion* never ceased to amaze me. Everything he did was motivated be these two virtues. He never put himself first. I am reminded of the saying, "if you want **JOY** you must put Jesus first, others second, and yourself last." This was his guiding principle.

Steve Land came to work with us at the Southside church. He and Kelland made a great team as they worked together to move the church forward. Their priority was to change and educate the mindset of the Southside people. Growth comes to those who believe that 'nothing is impossible.' The few loyal members had to be convinced that more blessings were in store for them. It took time, much prayer, and hard work to reap a harvest. But, God rewarded them for their earnestness and diligent work.

My sister, Lillian, lived in New Jersey. Her husband, Warren, was a good man but never made a commitment to the Lord. When it came to 'religion' he left that to Lillian and their two children. Faithfully, they were in church every Sunday. He didn't have time to go.

As the result of a serious accident that happened some years before, osteomyelitis (inflammation of the bone marrow, and often times flaking off of the bone) was making his left leg almost unbearable with pain. It seemed to get worse year after year. The doctors had placed a steel rod in that leg to support it when he walked. But, nothing seemed to ease his pain. This was one of the many times he was in the hospital. He was desperate. He didn't want to have his leg amputated. But, what else could he do? It seemed that the doctor's had done everything possible for him.

He told Lillian he believed the Lord would save him if Kelland came and prayed with him. She called, and Kelland was on the next flight north. After picking him up at Newark Airport they went straight to Warren's bedside at the hospital. They prayed, they cried, they rejoiced! From that day on my brother-in-law was a changed man. Until his death in 1974 he was a church-goer and a strong witness for his Lord. Praise the Lord!

We enjoyed our three and one-half years of growth during the pastorate at Southside Church in Atlanta and were not anxious to leave. State Overseer W.C. Byrd had approached Kelland to take the position of *Georgia's State Youth and Christian Education Director.* Reverend and Mrs. Ray Pace had served the state effectively for the past four years in this capacity. Kelland felt a younger man would be better for the job. He told Brother Byrd that he was flattered but maybe he should consider someone else for the job.

Several weeks had gone by and Brother Byrd asked Kelland again to accept the youth director position. He called Kelland with an 'r' in the name. "Kellard, I'm going to ask you once again to take the job as State Youth and Christian Education Director. I've prayed about this and feel you are the one for this time. I've never ask a man a second time to do anything but I think you are the one that the Lord wants at this time." Kelland listened to the man of God. He had confidence in Brother Byrd and felt he was a good man. By this time Kelland was rethinking the whole matter. After he came home and discussed it with me and the family, he got back with Brother Byrd and accepted. Of course, this would be subject to approval of the State Council which was unanimous.

When we left Southside to become Georgia's *State Youth and Christian Education Director* the church was averaging 350 in Sunday School. We are grateful for everything accomplished at the Southside church.

Philippians 4:4 *"Rejoice in the Lord always: and again I say, Rejoice"*.

MEMORABLE TRIBUTES FROM FAMILY AND FRIENDS

Steve Land

A Personal Appreciation: The Pastor of Joy

As all the other contributors to this volume of appreciative remembrance, I am pleased and honored to offer only a few anecdotes which, I hope, will allow you to sense the joy and blessing that it was to know this man.

Joy was the fruit of the Spirit that grew all over the tree of his life. That joy was contagious, and it strengthened those who came in contact with him. I believe that his joy was from the Lord and a key to his influence as a pastor, husband, father, and friend.

I came to know the Jeffords family in the late 1960's when they were serving the Southside Church of God in Atlanta, Georgia. I listened to the stories of dedicated service in tents and parsonages serving the body of Christ. Kelland and Nelia were a team that had worked hard, were deeply committed to and loved their work.

It was 1969. I had heard about the Jeffords from Paul L. Walker and others in the state of Georgia and, being single and a student at Candler Theological Seminary (Emory University), I was looking for a job. I had been working in a hospital as a psychiatric aide; but, since I had come to Atlanta to start an inner-city ministry (later called Mission Possible), I wanted to get some ministerial experience. After we had conversed for a while, Pastor Jeffords asked me to be his assistant pastor. I was to do pastoral visits, help clean the church, work with the youth and lead the choir from time to time - and, I would receive $100 per month! I was excited and eager to jump in and get going. Pastor Jeffords told me that we needed to change the thinking in the church by lovingly leading them to be a more inviting and receptive congregation. He was an enthusiastic, evangelistic pastor with a persistent vision for growth and a persuasive manner.

And he was patient. There was a lady in the church who led a weekly prayer time with some of the older sisters. Practically every Sunday, as Pastor Jeffords would stand in the pulpit and read the list of persons to be prayed for, this lady would wait till the last minute to say anything. Then, just when the pastor would begin to say, "Let us pray," she would interrupt and loudly, with her hand raised toward the pulpit, call out his name. "Brother Jeffords! Me and my ladies have some things we think we need to pray about!" The pastor would turn around, look at me, seated on the platform just behind him, and smile. Turning back to the congregation, with his sweetest smile he would softly say, "Yes, sister, go ahead." Everyone knew that he knew what was going on and that he was patiently and humorously indulging this lady.

He would also be courageous and confrontational. Two stores came to mind in this regard. The State Overseer of Georgia, a man of great strength and influence, came in with an agenda to split the state into northern and southern administrative areas. Brother Jeffords seemed to know practically every minister in the state; and, being from south Georgia while serving in the north, he thought that for the sake of fellowship, financial strength and evangelistic effectiveness, the state should not be split. While this was being debated, Brother Jeffords, serving on the State Council, was walking with the Overseer and a group of ministers from the State Office to their cars to go to lunch. In a lull in the conversation, Brother Jeffords put his hand on the Overseer's shoulder and said, "Brother, you are one of the greatest ministers in our church and you are so smart. In fact, I'd say you would be right almost all the time, but I'll be right a few times! And this is one of them!" Everyone, including the Overseer, burst out laughing at this good-natured but courageous advocacy.

This courage could be seen in the pastorate also. The pastor suspected that one of the ladies in the church was being abused. He asked me to go with him to visit the husband- a large powerful man known to drink a lot of beer, especially when he was relaxing at home. I was nervous as we knocked on the door. The man yelled at us to come on in, which we did...slowly. There sitting in his easy chair, surrounded by crushed beer cans, was this huge man. Brother Jeffords went right in and pulled up a chair next to the man. I stayed back a little. In a few minutes, Pastor had the man laughing so hard he was crying. Then, all of a sudden, Brother Jeffords' face turned red with anger as he put his finger in the man's face and yelled, "You're going to go straight to hell, if you keep on hurting your dear wife! We love you. Pray, Steve!" And I did pray a fervent prayer - with my eye partially open to make sure the man wasn't coming after both of us. He didn't. We prayed for a while, the man stopped hurting his wife, and eventually came to church with her.

Once we were sitting in a minister's meeting and Brother Jeffords not only knew the pastor who was preaching, he also knew the sermon. He would lean over and whisper to me, "He's going to laugh here. Now he's going to cry. Now he'll tell a story." It was hilarious, if somewhat distracting! But he had great love for this preacher. He could be blessed, see the seriousness and the humor in the divine-human undertaking we call ministry. It was serious fun.

He could be dramatic. One Sunday night he was preaching with all his might when an elderly gentleman, sitting on a front pew, fell asleep - as he had done before on several occasions. Without missing a beat in his sermon, Brother Jeffords came down from the preaching platform, sat in the man's lap and exclaimed to all, "We need to wake up in this church." The man awoke with start, Pastor hugged him and everyone laughed. He made his point to that man - and any others who may have been asleep with their eyes open.

A real key to this complex and hard-working man is his upbringing in south Georgia. Others in this volume have noted the deep roots of his family in the Church of God. The Jeffords home was a place of hospitality and care for pastors and others. And this was true of Brother and Sister Jeffords' parsonages throughout their ministry. I really enjoyed getting to know his Brother Raymond and his mother. She worked for years in a little post office and, as she had done for so many others, she prepared a meal for Brother Jeffords and me in one of our visits back to his home.

In later years I drove him back home, because his eyesight was weakening. Wherever we stopped along the way in restaurants, general stores, service stations- it didn't matter; wherever we stopped he knew everybody. His joy and hospitable spirit reached out to everyone and made his witness believable and caring.

My wife, Peggy, and I were married December 25, 1969 in Peggy's home church in Hemmingway, South Carolina. Brother and Sister Jeffords interrupted Christmas with their family to drive from Atlanta to Hemmingway to officiate and play for this wedding. He would kid us about sanctified love, kissing, and courtship. We were so blessed by the generous spirit and dedicated example of Kelland and Nelia Jeffords. I look forward to another wedding feast- soon, I hope. We will sit with him, his family, and all of God's family. Until then I pray that all of who knew him as well as all of you who read this book, will be inspired, convicted, and motivated to serve God with all your heart. And don't forget the example of this humble, joyful man. The beauty of God's holiness in our life is humility and the joy of the Lord is our strength. Remember this, remember Brother Jeffords, and be a blessing to those around you.

Steven Jack Land, Ph. D.
President/ Professor
Church of God Theological Seminary

Chapter 8

Serves As Georgia's Youth and Christian Education Director

At the 1970 General Assembly in St. Louis, Missouri Kelland was rushed to the hospital. He was suffering with a carbuncle on the back of the neck and the infection grew worse. By the time we arrived in St. Louis, he was a very sick man. I called down to the desk at the hotel and asked for an ambulance. Not knowing what hospital to ask for the ambulance driver took him to City Hospital. The hospital had been converted from a military hospital to one that indigent people of St. Louis would go. The rooms were wards with 15-20 beds in each section. Partitions of cloth provided the only privacy for the patient. Despite these deplorable accommodations, Kelland would not complain.

Instead, he found the patients to be quite amusing. There was this one elderly man, whose bed was adjacent to his and would start calling for the nurse every night about the same time. It was usually after his evening meal. His plea for assistance went something like this:

"Oh nurse, bedpan please." He would wait to see if the nurse was on her way. She didn't come. He calls again, "Oh, n-u-r-s-e, bedpan please." Again, waiting for the nurse, but she never came, he calls, "Oh, n-u-r-s-e, bedpan please." He was getting more impatient, with urgency in his voice, each time he called, "Oh, n--u--r--s--e, bedpan please." His voice was now shrill, very impatient and urgent. After calling out to the nurse for ten or more minutes, his final desperate call was….."t-o-o l-a-t-e, nurse," followed by a loud sound (?@!*/?) and sigh of relief…u-u--g-h, and unintelligible mumbling to himself. Finally, the nurse would come in and reprimand the old gentlemen with scolding remarks…."shame on you…you should be ashamed of yourself…look at you…what a mess…I can't believe you," as she cleaned him up and the unfortunate mess he created.

Kelland was laughing with sidesplitting laughter as this scenario repeatedly happened night after night. This was a story that he would repeat over and over for years to come. He would tell it in his high-pitched, expressive voice, and have those listening rolling with laughter. He could usually find humor wherever and whatever the circumstance.

Even with the disappointment of being hospitalized for the duration of the assembly, he found humor and would share with those who came to visit him at City Hospital. His optimistic outlook on life was an inspiration to us all.

Dianne had won State Teen Talent and was representing Georgia at the national finals. It was a happy time to see her win at national in piano, but we felt a bit of sadness because her dad could not be present. He was so proud of her and had given his total support. We had to face up to it and bade him bye at the St. Louis Airport. He had to be flown back to Atlanta and admitted to Northside Hospital. Dianne and I drove back to Atlanta by car.

This minor set back of sickness did not dampen Kelland's enthusiasm. He started making plans for his first State Youth Board meeting, which took place in his hospital room. He was soon out of the hospital, in the office, and getting his plans set for the year ahead.

He had read about a single church in another denomination that had given over $50,000 to the youth missions program. If one church could raise this kind of money for youth missions, surely the Churches of God in Georgia could, too.

In the Evangel an article written in tribute to him on September 28, 1987:

"He set in motion a new spirit for YWEA throughout the Church of God. No state in the Church of God had ever raised $20,000 for a project. Not only did he reach this goal, but he laid the foundation to reach $100,000."

For four consecutive years he was awarded a plaque in recognition of his outstanding work for Y.W.E.A. (Youth World Evangelism Appeal). Georgia was now the leader in youth missions giving. His vision, enthusiasm, and love for people continued to serve as a model for others to follow.

A statewide Sunday School Conference was planned during our tenure as State Director and held at Mt. Paran Church of God in Atlanta, Georgia. The theme for the conference was *"REACH OUT"* with four subheadings:

1. Reach Out in Hope...Dr. Cecil Knight
2. Reach Out in Faith...Dr. Paul L. Walker
3. Reach Out in Love...Rev. B. E. Underwood
4. Reach Out in Spirit...Rev. A.V. Childers

The Holy Spirit moved in the conference and challenged men's hearts to 'Reach Out" to those communities who were hurting and needed the love of the church. The sermon by Rev. B.E.Underwood, of the Pentecostal Holiness Church, spoke on the theme, *Reach Out In Love.* The audience fell to their knees crying and praying as he so passionately and graphically illustrated the story of Hosea and Gomer (Hosea 1:2-10). The tone was set for future growth in Sunday School growth and for Y.W.E.A. (Youth World Evangelism Appeal) as a result of this conference.

The song **Reach Out** was sung by a mass youth choir under the direction of F. M. Moore. Over and over again throughout the two day conference, we were challenged to reach out and touch the hearts of those who were less fortunate, and to those who needed a friend or someone who was all alone; even if it took walking that extra mile, letting Christ's love spill out in kindness to those who needed someone. Reach Out, Reach Out, Reach Out was emphasized in both song and sermon

REACH OUT IN LOVE

Rev. Dr. B. E. Underwood
Assistant General Overseer and
Executive Director of World Missions
Pentecostal Holiness Church

Introduction of Speaker: Rev. Kelland Jeffords, State Youth and Christian Director of Georgia

Response: Thank you Bro. Jeffords. It is a real delight for me to be in this session today.   I thoroughly enjoyed the week at Berchtesgaden (Germany) with the service men. And, on the way over there we stopped in England. I was preaching in a Pentecostal Holiness Methodist Church. The building was Methodist and the congregation was Pentecostal Holiness. They had rented it to us because they couldn't fill it....and, we had it full on Saturday night. And, I learned a song....now, I am not a song leader....and don't anybody get any ideas. I am not expecting anybody to invite me to lead singing at a camp meeting or anything like that. I quit that twenty-five years ago.

But, this little song got hold of me. Once in a while a song kind of captivates me because it says something. So many songs I hear these days make a good racket, they just don't say anything. But this song said something! And I carried it with me over to the retreat and got brave enough...for the first time in, I guess in twenty years, to teach anybody to sing except my grandchildren of somebody like that. And it kind of became a theme song for us...didn't it Brother Jeffords?

Now if these good musicians will help me. I have no idea what key it is in and if I did, I probably wouldn't start in that key. (Laughter) In fact, if you can find the key that I am going to sing it in on the piano you'll be lucky! Sometimes I sing in keys that aren't even on these instruments. It there are any dignitaries, I want you to crawl under the bench and get out of our way a few minutes. Because, I want everyone to sing it, not only with our lips, but with our hands because this is a sign language song! And, if any of you folks are so sophisticated and dignified that you can't do it, I want you to go off and hide somewhere. 'Cause we're going to embarrass you if you feel that way.

The song goes something like this and we'll start it in a minute...but, if I am yours and you are mine....or , I am His and He is mine and His banner over me is love.   I am yours and you are mine and His banner over me is love. How many of you have ever heard it? In a moment or two I want you folks to help me real good, and these musicians, I know they're experts...and they're going to land right where we are. And we are going to get started.   Have you heard it? (The pianist, Nelia Jeffords, calls out in the background, "yes, I was there"). Oh good! Wonderful!

His Banner Over Me Is Love

I am His and He is mine,
And His Banner over me is love.
I am His and He is mine.
And His Banner over me is love.
I am His and He is mine.
And His Banner over me is love,
His Banner over me is love.

I am yours and you are mine,
And, His Banner over us is love.
I am yours and you are mine,
And His Banner over us is love.
I am yours and you are mine,
And His Banner over us is love,
His Banner over us is love.

He lifts us up into heavenly places,
And His Banner over us is love.
He lifts us up into heavenly places,
And His Banner over us is love.

He lifts us up into heavenly places,
And His Banner over us is love,
His Banner over us is love.

Some of you folks are a little slow and didn't catch on. (Laughter)
But, by now you have caught on and I want us to sing it one more
time. And, when we get to that second verse...you know, we forget
this sometimes. Everywhere I go among Pentecostal Holiness folks,
you Church of God people have already been delivered from it; but,
you can help me I guess. I find people with all kinds of yardsticks
that they run around measuring folks about their religion. Jesus gave
one that is the best I know. He said, "That by this, shall all men
know that you're my disciples." Why? Because <u>you love one
another.</u> You have love one for another.

Now, there are a lot of good holiness folks that have a lot of things
for one another, but love is not one of them. And I want us on this
Friday morning to sing this song and let the love of God be shed
abroad in our hearts. You know it know! And, I want everyone to
sing is. Come on! You folks that were afraid you were going to
make a mistake...a lot of cowards in the world....until they can do it
perfectly, they won't try. But you know it now! And, so come on
and join us. And when we get to the second verse, I want you to turn
around to the person next to you and sing to him. (Laughter) And
you husbands, it wouldn't hurt you to sing to your wife. She
probably would like to hear that...it may have been a long time.
Amen? All right!

(Piano begins playing in background...the entire congregation begins
singing His Banner Over Me is Love).   Halleluiah...Glory to God!
(Everyone is praying aloud and praising God!)

Our Father, we thank you for the love of God. We thank you because Jesus has made us aware that God is love....may our hearts be strangely warmed today...of that Love of God being shed abroad in our hearts. And grant, our Father, as we gather about by thy word that the Holy Spirit may seize us afresh with that God-like quality that makes us love the unlovable, and the unlovely, and those who are hostile to us and who are enemies to the cause of Christ...may we love them as Jesus loved...that men may know God as He really is...because it is in Jesus name we pray. Amen.

I want to read from the prophesy of Hosea...the first chapter, beginning with verse 2. And I want to speak to you...the subject is, *Reach Out In Love.* I am going to start with a broken hearted God.

Hosea

Chapter 1: 2-10

2. The beginning of the word of the Lord by Hosea. And the Lord said to Hosea, Go take thee a wife whoredoms and children of whoredoms; for the land hath committed great whoredom, departing from the Lord.
3. So he went and took Gomer the daughter of Diblaim; which conceived, and bare him a son.
4. And the Lord said unto him, Call his name *Jezreel;* for yet a little while, and I will avenge the blood of Jezreel upon the house of Jehu, and will cause to cease the kingdom of the house of Israel.
5. And it shall come to pass at that day, that I will break the bow of Israel in the valley of Jezreel.
6. And she conceived again, and bare a daughter. And God said unto him, Call her name *Lo-ruhamah;*   for I will no more have mercy upon the house of Israel; but I will utterly take them away.
7. But I will have mercy upon the house of Judah, and will save them by the Lord their God, and will not save them by bow, nor by sword, not by battle, by horses, nor by horsemen.
8. Now when she had weaned Lo-ruhamah, she conceived, and bare a son.
9. Then said God, Call his name *Lo-ammi:* for ye are not my people, and I will not be your God.
10. Yet the number of the children of Israel shall be as the sand of the sea, which cannot be measured or numbered; and it shall come to pass, that in the place where it was said unto them, Ye are not my people, there it shall be said unto them, Ye are the sons of the living God.

May God bless to our heart, the reading of his eternal word.

The prophet Hosea, a prophet of the northern kingdom of Israel for seventy long years, prophesized to a backslidden, paganized people of God. In fact, longer that any of the other writing prophets of the Old Testament, Hosea was called upon to preach to a rebel people. He preached, prophesized, at least a part of his ministry, during the reign of Jeroboam the II. It was a time when people had a form of religion; they worshipped God in the morning and Baal in the afternoon. Open and disgusting vies and debauchery was the order of the day. God's people had so backslidden and fallen away from their faithfulness to Him they could only be classified only as a nation of whoredom or harlotry. She had played the harlot against God...had violated every law that he had given her; had sinned against His love. Had broken every vow and every covenant...and God said, "Ye are no longer my people". And He called upon Hosea to go and minister to these people.

In fact, the day of Hosea was much like our own day and our own nation. We can draw many parallels this morning. But there was a strange difference between Hosea and any other prophet of God in the bible. I've never been able to understand how critical scholars can read the bible, and come up with a dichotomy of the picture of God in scripture....thinking that the God of the Old Testament, is a God of judgment, and a God of righteous...who knows no love. For the God of the New Testament is a God of love....for no where in all of holy scripture, outside of Mount Calvary itself, is God revealed in his broken hearted love for man like he is in the book of Hosea. The story here is the story of God imparting to a preacher, a super natural love that none of us naturally possess. In fact, the story in the natural is the story of a preacher's broken heart...and a preacher's broken home.

A young man called to preach encountered a beautiful young girl....her name was *Gomer*. That means *complete or perfect*. I really think that Gomer was probably the most beautiful woman in all of Israel. If they'd had a Miss Israel contest, I think Gomer would have won hands down. I think she was so beautiful and so complete...in every way, that this young preacher thought, what more beautiful woman could I ever find to be my wife in this ministry to which God has called me. I know there are preachers, I have heard them preach, that God told him to marry a harlot. I don't believe a word of that. You can believe it if you want to. You see, Hosea is writing as an old man. He's looking back on the thing God did give him permission to marry Gomer....and God knew what she was going to be....this is part of God's school for Hosea. But, I think when Hosea fell in love with her; she was everything that a young Israelite would have wanted as a wife.

Of course, I know that this would immediately turn some folk off. For I learned over thirty years ago, when I started preaching, that some people think that a preacher ought to have a wife as ugly as he can find. (a few seconds gap in the recording) I started preaching before I got married, and you'd never believe some of the things that were picked out for me...to be my bride! (laughter)   Almost everywhere I went somebody had chosen some choice maiden of Israel for me. (more laughter) And in my innocence and ignorance, I often times would find myself seated at a table where I had been invited to a sumptuous meal, and realized I was not there because I was as a prophet of God....I was there because I was a prospect. (laughter)

I guess there may be still people who feel that way, but there is nothing in the bible that would have criticized Hosea one time for choosing this beautiful girl. And, he loved her as much as any man has ever loved a woman in this world I suppose. And this young prophet of God gave himself totally to this beautiful maiden of Israel. But you see Gomer had, because of her beauty, and her wide experience in the society of Israel had learned and enjoyed good things, bright lights, and good times...and the preacher's salary and circumstances didn't provide for much of that. And slowly but with deadly certainty, Hosea discovered that Gomer was drifting away from his ministry. And I don't suppose there is anything more tragic in all of the world, than for a man of God to have a wife whose heart drifts from him and does not share his ministry.

The older I get, the more I realize that one of the greatest blessings God ever gave me was a wife who loved God and was willing to bare the burden of the ministry that God placed upon my shoulders. And, when she had to be mom and dad both to teenagers while I was gone two-thirds to three-fourth's of the time, I thank God that she had something of a call, that kept her there and kept her love true, and faithful, and loyal; and not only to God, but to me. Sure a preacher needs that! A preacher without that is in a lonely place in this world. (yes, amen)

Hosea, a prophet of God, as the days went by drew increasingly worse, there was a son born and already the seeds were being sown. God said call him *"Jezreel"* or God will sow. And, judgment was coming. She conceived again, bore a daughter, and God said call her *"Lo-ruhamah"*....which means un-pitied or unloved. I think that Lo-ruhamah was probably the most neglected girl in all of the community where Hosea lived. You could see her most any day after she was about 6...9 months old on the porch playing, maybe out with Jezreel....dirty, unkempt, and uncared for. Mom would take off and be gone for hours at first, and then later she would go and be gone for days....and unless the prophet were there, little Lo-ruhamah was the most uncared for little child in all the community.

But, then Gomer would come back after two or three days of being gone, and tell some unlikely story and Hosea wanting to believe the best, would always take her back. Things went on like that for a while until there was another child born. I don't really think that Hosea knew what was happening completely, until this third child was born. And God said you call him *"Lo-ammi"*...which means no child of mine. And, I think for the first time the revelation of God had dawned on Hosea, that this child was not his and didn't belong to him anyway. This was the child of someone else. And all along until Gomer had bee gone for days and sometimes weeks in coming back and he'd take her back. People didn't understand. The neighbors talked.

They'd come to Hosea and say, "Hosea, I don't want to be gossiping; but, I am your friend and I think you ought to know." You know folks haven't changed much...people have been the same in about every generation. Some good interested neighbor, I'm sure came and said that I thought you ought to know that I saw Gomer down at the market today. You know there came in with a caravan of goods this morning and I saw her down there; and she really was having a great time with one of the traders from the East. I though you might like to know that. Of course, those there by this time already knew a little of that. And then there came a day when she didn't come back. And, after a day or two he began to investigate.

And, somebody said, "Well, I saw her leaving with the caravan the other day and it looked like she was leaving for good". And she stayed gone for a week, and two weeks, and for a month. And soon Hosea decided that this woman to whom he had given all of his love had deserted him; and left him with those three children and run off with her lovers. If it had been me, I think I should have marked her off. I would have scriptural grounds....had every right legally. He had every right to throw her overboard.   And, as far as I am concerned to re-marry... the only purpose for a divorce was a right to re-marry. Of course, I am not going to get into that....that's not your problem. I fight it enough in my own communion without yours. (laughter) But he had every legal right to divorce. There's no reason that he shouldn't have thrown her over-board...but, he didn't.

In fact, the life of Hosea from here on was lived with long weary nights of sobbing, searching, prayer as he asked God, "Is there something I could have done that I didn't do?" "Is there anything that I failed in, if I could have Lord...I want you to forgive me". As you read in this book of Hosea, and you hear God crying out...and saying, "Oh Ephraim, how can I give you up?" You can read between that and you can hear Hosea as he sobs and cries in the midnight hour and says, "Oh Gomer, how can I let you go? I know that you are yonder with some other lover...but Gomer, I still love you and I want you to come home....and if you come back, there is a place for you here". I don't understand and I'll have to admit, and you don't either....we would not have done that. The neighbors must have said to Hosea, "You ought to be glad Gomer's gone!" It's good riddance to be rid of her.

Ah...a few years ago I had a young preacher...I don't think I ever experienced anything quite like this...but, I had a young man...I've know him since he was just a boy. And he has been a good boy, as far as I know, all his life. But he married a "she-devil" for a wife...that's the sorriest woman I've about ever known. And time and again I went with him one night off to a night club, way off back in an area that nobody except criminals and scoundrels would go...to find his wife where she had gone to meet one of the sorriest characters in that part of the world...and over and over again.

And, one day he came to me, I was a superintendent, he said, "Bother Underwood, I don't know what I am going to do...those four children, I've got to do something!" He said, "I came home the other day," and said, "my wife had brought in this peddler of pornography. And in my house, in my living room, with my little children....they had shown the vilest films that you can get to show on the screen in front of my children; and she had sat there and made love to that sorry rascal." He said, "I want you to help me get my children in an orphanage somewhere....I've got to do something about it." And, I said, "Alright." And I took him and we got the children a place to go...and I said, "Tom, you ought to be glad you're rid of her...you ought to be glad it's over! She's not fit to be a preacher's wife, anybody's wife....be glad she is gone!"

She paraded his name in the newspaper, full-page, as she went out to play for a nightclub...and announced the fact that she had learned music in the church...and been brought up in the home and disgraced and brought reproach on everything that he had represented. But there he was, about six weeks later, he came back, and I sat dumbfounded as he said, "Brother Underwood, she came back, and she says that she wants to try again...she wants us to go get the children." And he said, "I love her and I'm going to take her back." And I said, "You don't mean that!" And he said, "Yes, I do...if she will just live for God...I'll be glad for her to be my wife until I die." And I said, "Man, you've got something that I don't have....I don't believe I could ever feel like that...YOU"VE got a deeper love than I've ever known, I believe." But sobbing there, we prayed together and I helped him go get the children. And the same thing happened over again...they were gone again. But, he still loved her.

This is exactly the experience of Hosea. Hosea never said a word about Gomer. The children would say, "Oh, I know"...you know children....if you ever doubt the fallen nature of man, you just watch how children treat one another. Hallelujah! And I can imagine some of them meeting Jezreel, he was getting up in years, now old enough to know. And they'd say, "Now Jezreel, where' your mother?" And he'd say, "Well, she's gone." "Where is she, Jezreel?" (There'd be a tittering, a little laughter, giggling in the crowd). Jezreel said, "Well, I don't know, but she is coming back." " When is she coming back...Jezreel?" "I don't know, but daddy said she was coming back."

But every night when they'd pray, he'd gather them around and he'd say, "Children, momma's comin' back....let's pray that God would bring momma back home." And, they'd pray together. And with all the courage that a man can muster in an impossible situation like that, he'd put the children to bed. And little Lo-ruhamah might cry and say, "Daddy, I want my momma." And he would say, "Well, sweetheart, you go to bed and maybe momma will come back tomorrow." That had gone on, and on, and on, but he never let her go. Never once did he tell them about the sordid and awful wretched life the momma lived. There was always hope. And, when they were in bed, how his pillow must have burned with hot tears as he wept and sobbed and said, "Oh, God! I can't let her go, please bring her back."

And he kept praying until the day came. And probably that same neighbor came by and said, "Hosea, guess what I saw today? You'll never believe what I saw today; I almost missed it! It's been several years now, but I came by the slave market. They're going to have an auction tomorrow. I was looking over, you see I lost one of my best slaves and I need a good strong man. I was looking them over and I passed by a wretched hunk of humanity...that's the only one that attracted my attention. I thought, "who in the world would ever want anything like that?" It looked like a worn out old woman...that wasn't worth, well...she'd be more trouble to keep, than she would be any help in the home. And they've got her down at the slave market. And I...I'ah looked, and you know what? When I looked at her, I thought there was something familiar and I got to checking...and guess who it was? They've got Gomer down at the slave market and they're going to try to auction her off. Boy, you ought to be glad you got rid of her. If you'd see her now, you'd be glad she's gone. She's not worth having as a slave, much less, as a wife and a mother." Hosea said, "Thank you" and went home.

And, I can imagine he got those children together and he said, "Children, I want us to get ready and get the house cleaned up...get everything ready. I want us to clean it like it's never been cleaned....and I want it 'spic and span' because momma's coming home tomorrow. And with those children they cleaned and fixed that house until everything was 'spic and span'. He put them off to bed and then went out and measured up all the barley that he had. He counted his money ...he only had 15 pieces of silver...he wasn't sure that would be enough. He gathered up all the grain...it was a homer and a half...about 14 bushels of barley. He got it all sacked up and ready early the next morning before daybreak. If you could have seen the preacher dressed in his best...with a little ole bag by his side, full of all the money he had, and a beast of burden, with all the grain that he had...he was going down toward the slave market.

He got to the market and, of course, they are saving the rubbish 'til last...and he stands there all day long. People are wondering what the Prophet is doing there. They bid on strong, star ward men and beautiful, attractive, strong women who can be slaves...but the Prophet doesn't bid not one dollar, not one piece of silver for them. And, after long in the afternoon they bring out this hunk of wretched humanity...flesh and bones. Wrinkled together around an outcast that has been thrown off by her lover...that's what sin always does. There are a lot of people like that in our world. Unlovely pieces of humanity that is ready for the trash heap. And from every outward appearance they are not worth fooling with.

And, when they started bidding, Hosea stepped up and probably started off with five pieces of silver. And they had some kind of *baiter* there I'm sure, and he saw he was anxious to buy. And he began to bid against him to bring it up and they took it up to ten...and twelve...and thirteen. Hosea bid fifteen pieces if silver and they saw he was anxious. He didn't know about this bidding business. He was anxious to get the woman back. He didn't learn to negotiate too well. The man bid sixteen before Hosea could tell him and then, I could see the ole' Prophet as he goes up to the auctioneer and he says, "Sir, I don't know how much this man is willing to give," but he said, "I want that woman...I want her more that I want anything in this world. I don't have anymore silver...but, I got fourteen bushel of barley. And, if you'll let me have her, I will give you fifteen pieces of silver and that fourteen bushel of barley...that's all I got." And the auctioneer probably nodded to the baiter out there and he finally gave the bid to Hosea.

And Hosea walks over, like a mother taking a hurt child. He takes those shackles off the legs and the hands of this wasted, reprobate of a woman. He takes them all out of his pouch be his side and puts it over those broken places in her skin. Those sores that have been put there by those shackles...rubs them very tenderly, like a mother would a baby. And, he takes that hunk of humanity by the arm, with everybody gazing and looking on, he said, "Come on honey, let's go home. You're going to be mine from now on. And, you're never going to leave anymore." And they walk up the road with the whole crowd looking and wondering what on earth is wrong with that man's mind. <u>There was nothing wrong with his mind, there was just something right with his heart.</u> You see...this is the picture of God. This is what God is trying to say to Israel...and to you and me. And if you read the last verse in this book of Hosea....it says, *that men of wisdom ought to learn by this lesson of Hosea.*

This is God...that's how he found me. I wasn't worth having sir. I wasn't worth fooling with! I should have been marked off and left alone. But, He bid high for me; He gave everything He had. He said, "I want him! I want that boy! I want him!" (People are giving shouts of praise). You see, this is the way we can R*each Out In Love.* This love of God called upon us to manifest the supernatural. And all of us should know this love...this world would never be saved. I know we look at the world around us....we are masters at returning their hostility. The world hates the church...the bible says that. But, the Lord tells us we are suppose to love the world...the only trouble is we've learned to return the vile pious brand of hostility; the hostility of the world and they have no idea that God loves them.

But sir, I want you to know that the church of people like
Gomer...that's what we make saints out of. (Yeah...amen) If you are
looking for a respectable society...I find people occasionally who
want the church to be a respectable society.....where people can
come and be proud they're a member.   Sir, I got news for
you....you're in the wrong crowd. You don't want to be a member of
my church.   You had better go look to the Kiwanis Club, or the
Lions Club, or someplace else.   You don't need to come to my
church. For my church is made up of a motley crowd. Oh, it's a
motley crowd that's in this church!   Respectable...not on your
life...It's a *redeemed society*...but, it's not a *respectable society.*

In fact, one of the first leaders we had, one of the pioneers, I guess
we ought to turn him out of the church...cause everybody knew, it
was public knowledge that he cursed, used profanity; he even denied
he had anything to do with us. We should have turned him out...I
guess we would have, but he repented.   Since we are a loving,
tenderhearted, we took him back in and put him up at the next
general convention and he preached. Can you imagine that? Didn't
even take his license away from him and he got up and preached;
three thousand people got saved.

Two of our leading writers were scoundrels and rascals; our greatest
missionary, scared more people out of becoming Christians than
anybody we ever had in the whole history of our church.   In fact,
when he got religion, people were so afraid of him because he put so
many people in jail and caused the death of so many....until they
didn't even take him in; but we always got some people that got big
hearts like Jesus. They brought him and introduced him, and we
were embarrassed not to take him: We took him in before we knew
it, they'd already ordained him as a missionary and he's out starting
churches. We let him go.

One of our best evangelists we've got, we found him naked in a
cemetery. Everybody knew that God could tame him, put handcuffs
on him and couldn't hold him; he'd break them every time....but, he
met the head of the church one day, and He spoke a word of
deliverance to him. And, he put clothes on, and came and applied
for a license; and we sent him out to preach. And he became the

main preacher in one our districts. If you're looking for respectably, sir, you're looking in the wrong place.

If you come to my church, it's just likely you ladies, bless your hearts, you may want sophistication and respectability, and you never thought you better go somewhere else....I don't want you to be embarrassed. Because if you come to my church, you go to the women's auxiliary meeting, we got one there...she's one of the most active members. She had five husbands and God only knows how many others she lived with that didn't bother to marry her. But one day, one day...she met the head of the church and decided she loved this Jesus that we worship and we took her in. Before we could have a conference and decide what to do with her, she went out and pioneered a church. We took it in, in spite of the objections of some the people.

And sir, if you may come into the Sunday School class, you may bring that sweet little darling child of yours...and, one of the teachers in the junior department that might teach that little angel that bring to Sunday School, used to have seven devils...notorious for that; but, she said she got saved and we took her in and gave her a Sunday School class.

And if you go to the choir, you will probably be singing right beside a fellow that was on public welfare....he has a wonderful voice; I guess suffering brought that. He lived off of public welfare...full of sores; everybody shunned him because he was so obnoxious. He'd make you almost vomit to just look at him, but one day we found him...that's what we make church members out of (he laughs). We got hold of him and took him in the church! You see if you are looking for respectably, you're looking in the wrong place! The church is not a place for respectable people... it's a place for redeemed sinners!

It doesn't make a difference how far gone they may have been. God can get hold of them you see. No wonder the apostle said, *"I am praying that God will help you to comprehend what is the height, and depth, and length, and breathe the love of God."* Oh, this is the boundary of God's love has never been marked out. I couldn't tell you about it! For you see that the length of His love reaches back beyond the kin of history. You'll have to dig into the dusty books of history and then back beyond that. God's love reaches in activity in divine redemption. It reaches and leads down across the eternities beyond the vision of any prophet...you'll have to use your imagination to follow the love of God. The depth reaches down to the doorstep of hell, builds a rescue mission...right at the door of hell and snatches reprobates from the brands of burning. And, it reaches right up to the heavenlies...the throne of God. This love, a boundary of which has never been marked out, is the kind of love that God wants to put in your heart and mine. That the ten millions of people across this southeastern United States and the millions around this world, that are lost hunks of humanity, that are nothing but fuel for the fires of hell, as far as human reasoning is concerned can be loved as Hosea loved Gomer...and like God loves sinners.

You see, the great difference between Jesus and me....sometimes I get a little, like most folks do, and I get to thinking, Lord I am doing pretty good. I've been a Christian for thirty years. Lord, I don't smoke. I don't drink, and you know I get to thinking Lord; I thank you...I thank you! I get a little like those Pharisees did...I stand up beside Jesus; Publicans and sinners, they loved him. He was a friend of sinners. And, I like to be a friend of saints; I don't much like being the friend of sinners. Drunkards...who wants to be a friend of a drunkard, and a harlot, and a reprobate? And I get to standing up beside Jesus and I feel so little. I feel like crawling under the bench and saying, "God, I am not like Jesus. I am nothing like Jesus...you're going to have to do something with me." But sir, this is it. God didn't send us into the world to condemn the world. Jesus said, "the Son of Man came not to condemn the world", the world is already condemned....it's been under condemnation; that is not our job. Then He said, "that the world through me might be saved."

There are a lot of people out there this morning that would be thrilled beyond words if they knew how much God loved them. And God's depending on you and me to get the word to them; not in word only, but in deed and in truth. Some of you have got loved ones...have you ever traveled the road of loving somebody? Do everything in your power for them...and, like Gomer, they turn and follow the filthy and unclean, and the vile, and the sinful. And you trail and follow them, and love them, and do your best. And pretty soon, you get resentful, and you want to go, "God, what's wrong?"

And, I don't know about you, but I feel desperately this morning that I need to stand up to the cross, and say: "God, God so now let the love of Calvary flow out of the heart of the Son of God into my heart, that I can love people that are in the same position I was in when God found me." You see, we forget what we were and we ought not to forget. I want everybody here...I want everybody here...who really feels like I do and you want God this morning; if you don't feel you need it, you feel comfortable as you are, you just stay seated. Don't be troubled. But, if there is and sense of disturbance in your soul, that you say, "God, I need that...I don't have that like I need it." I want you to get on your feet right now...get to your feet. If you want God, if you're ready for God...you see, if you don't mean business it might be costly.

A lady was in a service like this and was challenged and she stood and said, "God, I'll do what you want me to do. I'll manifest your love to anybody anywhere if you'll just let me do it." She went home. The Lord started talking to her. He said, "I want you to get up early in the morning and I want you to go down to such and such a house." And, he called attention to the most disreputable place in all the city she lived. He said, "I want you to tell the madam that runs that house about Jesus." She said, "But Lord I can't go down there....what would people think if I go there?" He said, "I thought you told me that you would do whatever I wanted you to do." And, after a night of wrestling in prayer, she got up the next morning with fire under her arm and frightened almost out of her wits....and whimpered her way down to the most disreputable and vile place that she knew anything about. She got there, looking around, wondering and hoping that nobody saw her. She walked up to the door and knocked on the door. A lady, older than her years, marked with sin, still with her bathrobe on, came to the door. She looked at her and says, "Lady, what are you doing here? You are at the wrong place." She says, "No, I'm not at the wrong place....God sent me." She said, "But do you know where you are?" She said, "Yes, I know where I am." She said, "God sent me to tell you that he loves you and he wants you to be his child." Then that lady at the door broke down sobbing and the woman ran into the room and there together she told her about Jesus...and put her arm around this wretched fallen woman. She told her about Jesus and she gave her heart to God...and they went all over the house gathering up the girls who were there and bringing them down for this woman to tell about Jesus. And there that morning God in His mercy reached a segment of humanity that most people will never reach.

If you don't mean business, I say to you, you better not play games with God. Because God has love for some people in Atlanta that some of you wouldn't want to be seen with unless God helps you. But if you really mean it, I want you to slip out from where you are, and come and meet me around this altar. I want us to stand as close together, about as close to God as we can. And I want us to ask God to let something of Calvary's love flow into our hearts this morning to send us out of here to do God's will in the lost world. Hallelujah!

People aren't you glad God loves us? Aren't you glad he loved us, not when we were good, but when we were sinners? We didn't deserve it, but He loved us. And, what He is inviting us to do....is to share that love and communicate it to other people. I have the strange feeling this morning that God's going to do something in some of your hearts; it's going to send you out of here to a ministry that you probably didn't dream of before this service. If you'll let God speak to you now...I want you to lift your heart to God. And, I want us to ask the Lord right now, to come into our hearts and shed this love abroad in us as he alone can do. Everybody...Oh, Jesus....Oh, Jesus, Jesus, Jesus, Jesus...we love you this morning. Oh, we love you Lord because you first loved us...and we need you to touch us this morning with a sample of that divine love, with a portion of the divine compassion for a lost world. And, we pray that you will. God have moms to love wayward daughters, and daddies to love wayward sons; husbands to love wayward wives and love lost sinful strangers, Lord.

(Music begins playing in the background)

Alright, I want you to listen to me just a minute now...I want you for a moment to think about that loved one, that member of your family, or that close friend who has betrayed you more than any other and grieves you deeper more than anyone else: because of their sins and their waywardness. That person, if there is one whom you've marked off the list and you decided God, he is not worth fooling with anymore; and that you just about quit praying for...you don't want him around he's so far gone. I want you for a moment this morning...it might have been a long time since anyone reached out to him. It might be that he's gone far enough now, that like Gomer, and the slavery of sin has gotten a hold of him. And it might be now, more than all of his life, he's needed somebody to *Reach Out In Love.* And, if there is somebody like that in your family, your acquaintance; that child, that brother, that sister....I want you right now to focus your heart and your love upon that person. And say, "Jesus loved me through them. Help me to love them in spite of what they've done." In spite of everything, God help me to Reach Out and Love them, and don't let me cut them off Lord, before you cut them off. Let my patience be as long as yours, and let my love reach as far as your love reaches. Will you do that for just a moment? Just fix your mind upon that person...Reach out to that one person whom the Lord brings to your heart right now. Reach out to Him. Reach out to Him with all your heart.

(Piano and Organ begins playing song: Reach Out)

Hallelujah! Thank you Jesus for helping us. Thank you Lord for sharing a little of yourself with us. Thank you Jesus. God Bless you....I appreciate your warm reception to the message this morning. May God bless you real good.

Closing Prayer: Rev. Clarence Busby, Sr., State Secretary-Treasurer of Georgia

Later that summer in the Senior High Youth Camp a record album, entitled *"Reach Out"*, was recorded at LeFevre Studios in Atlanta. Proceeds from the sale of the record album were given to Y.W.E.A.

Another emphasis for Y.W.E.A. was statewide rallies. He and the *Churchmen Trio* traveled across the state of Georgia promoting youth missions. Georgia had not been divided at this time. Through his vision for Youth World Evangelism Appeal, many miles were traveled raising money for this worthwhile endeavor. He loved Georgia's youth. No sacrifice was too great for the young people of his beloved state of Georgia and the Church of God.

We spent every summer for twenty-two years working in youth camps in some capacity. Either as counselor, Bible teacher, director of music, night watchman, crafts, night speaker, we were there teaching, molding, and motivating young people to live for Christ.

He had a generous spirit and wanted youth campers to have a good time during their stay. It broke his heart if someone had spending money stolen, lost it, or if they overspent. I don't think I'm exaggerating when I say that in youth camp he gave away hundreds of dollars to those little darlings. They loved him and his generosity.

CHURCH OF GOD, GEORGIA STATE CAMP GROUND

Georgia State Council and State Overseer Paul F Henson

Kelland and Nelia
Floyd Timmerman – State Overseer
Georgia Campground – 1973

Kelland Jeffords
State Youth Work

Kelland and Nelia
Georgia Campground

**Kelland and Nelia
No. Ga. Mountains**

State Youth Board
Front Row: State Dir. Kelland Jeffords, Danny May, Elmer Golden, Jr., H.D.Spivey
Back Row: Billy Wilson, Harold Jones, Terry Guyton, Robert Herrin

Georgia State Council and State Overseer W.C. Byrd

Kelland and Nelia @ Rudersburg, Germany
European Bible Seminary

**Nelia and Kelland @ The Eagle's Nest
Berchtesgaden, Germany**

Kelland and Nelia in Athens, Greece
Atop The Acropolis near The Parthenon

MEMORABLE TRIBUTES FROM FAMILY AND FRIENDS

KELLAND K. JEFFORDS

by

MARCUS D. LAMB

I first heard of Kelland Jeffords when he served as State Youth and Christian Education Director for the Church of God in Georgia.

He was very innovative and ahead of his time as it related to different programs to reach youth.

I remember Kelland Jeffords as always being very enthusiastic and positive. He truly had the joy of the Lord and it was his strength.

The first Youth Camp that I attended as a young teenager was at the Church of God Campground in Doraville, Georgia, an Atlanta suburb. Kelland Jeffords was over that Youth Camp. It was fun but had boundaries, yet it had a great spiritual emphasis and many young people were touched by the Holy Spirit, including me.

Just a few years later, Brother Jeffords came to preach at my home church, which was the Shurlington Church of God in Macon, Georgia for my Pastor J .E. Thornton. The message was excellent. After the service I was invited to go out to eat with Brother Jeffords and Brother Thornton. While in the restaurant, I asked Brother Jeffords, "how you could know for sure that God had called you to preach?" He gave me a very clear and encouraging explanation. That meant a lot to me that an important Church Official like him would take the time to share with a young person like me.

A few months later, I surrendered to the ministry. I then entered Lee College. A couple of years after I was there, Pastor Kelland Jeffords became Senior Pastor of the Mableton Church of God in the Atlanta area. He invited me to drive down and hold a weekend revival at his church.

What a great time we had. His church had several hundred people and had continued to grow. There was wonderful worship in the services and a great Youth Choir led by his wife, Nelia. The Youth Group was led by Jim Bolin who now serves as the Senior Pastor of Trinity Chapel Church of God, Powder Springs, Georgia. As a result, there was a mighty outpouring of the Holy Spirit that weekend. I may have gotten more out of it than the church did. Also, the fellowship with Pastor Kelland and Nelia Jeffords and their children, Dianne, Keith and Danita, during meals at their home was priceless.

In 1980, I had the pleasure of riding with Pastor Jeffords and his family from Atlanta, Georgia to the Church of God General Assembly in Dallas, Texas. What a fun trip! Today, our Daystar Television Network is headquartered in Dallas.

In the mid 1980's, Kelland Jeffords was Senior Pastor of the Rainbow Drive Church of God in Decatur, Georgia. It was my privilege to introduce to Pastor Jeffords, my dear friend, the legendary Evangelist G. B. McDowell from Dallas, Texas who then conducted a great revival at Rainbow Drive that influenced people from around the Atlanta metro area.

In conclusion, Kelland Jeffords loved people. He had a heart for God and was particularly anointed to reach young people. He was a blessing to me and I will never forget him.

Marcus D. Lamb
President/CEO
Daystar Television Network

REFLECTIONS OF REVEREND KELLAND JEFFORDS

BY: RAY DAWSON

August 17, 2006

I am so happy to put down on paper my memories of Bro. Jeffords. As I begin this little project, a flood of emotions came washing over me. I am stopped in my tracks and made to remember how much this patriarch meant to my life and ministry.

Brother Jeffords had a subtle, but powerfully influential way about him. His mannerism was so easy to enjoy, one often didn't register the depth of his wisdom until later reflection. If you will, Brother Jeffords could sneak more meaningful thoughts into a short conversation than most can when sitting down for lengthy dialogue with the intent of brain-storming. He could insert a homespun cliché' into any situation that would bring laughter, and at the same time closure.

I have long wished to imitate Brother Jeffords' way of bringing laughter through tears, and tears through laughter. He always seemed to know just the right amount of humorous and serious approach to bring to anything. Often people are known as either funny or serious, but few times does a person have the balance of both. Brother Jeffords was seriously funny, but definitely serious about the right things at the right time.

Many years ago now, Sister Jeffords did something I will just call, "discover me." Before this sounds as if it lacks the proper humility, let me explain what it means. I was a young boy when Sister Nelia heard me singing in a choir and pulled me out to sing a solo part. I don't think, as I look back, she just heard a voice because we have had, and have now, many great vocalists in the Church of God. I have always believed she saw the hand of God on my life, and hopefully, the gift of the anointing. The way this applies to Brother Jeffords is, as I found out later, in the quiet way he had also observed me. At this time, though he was always nice to me, I thought maybe he just saw a rambunctious camper. During these days, Brother Jeffords was the State Youth Director for the churches of God in Georgia. Being such, he was an important person in the lives of many young people. More than once he had kept me from being kicked out of camp for mischief and being sent home.

A few years after Sister Jeffords had called me out for music, Brother Jeffords had perceived that God had called me out for ministry. This knowledge became very unnerving to me, as at the time, I had my life all planned out. The plan I had did not include preaching, though I too knew I was called, I had no intention of accepting this call. I was newly married to a beautiful, young wife and we were getting along with our lives. I was succeeding in keeping everyone unaware of my call, except my father-in-law, and you guessed it, Brother Kelland Jeffords.

"Every time an occasion would bring me into Brother Jeffords' presence, he would gently, lovingly harass me about knowing I had the call of God on my life to preach His Word. Brother Jeffords would always put it in the form of a question, with his voice rising to a high pitch, as only he could do. "Ray, Son," he would say, "Are you sure God is not calling you to preach?" He didn't know I would go home and weep because the call haunted me, and he reminded me I was not successfully hiding it. Soon enough, I did accept God's call on my life and it obviously gave great pleasure to Brother Jeffords. Now every time he would see me, he would say, rising to the same high pitch, "Ray, Son, I told you didn't I." I would just say, "Yes Sir," and then go off grumbling at God about why He had to tell Brother Jeffords about calling me.

This was the kind of watchful eye Brother Jeffords had on people, even young people, and also why he was loved and respected so. I learned so much from watching Him in so little time. He illustrated to me how to be serious about your business, but never let the fun go out of life. His humor is so invested now in his son, Keith, that every time I'm around him, I am reminded of Brother Jeffords' influence. To whoever reads this meager effort, just know that Kelland Jeffords still lives through those who remember!

Remembering A True Saint,

Ray Dawson

Chapter 9

Mableton Welcomes The Jeffords

We were assigned to Mableton Church of God when our four-year statute of limitations for Youth and Christian Education Director of Georgia was over. The Mableton people welcomed us with much excitement. During our pastorate, we would again go through remodeling of the church with additional rooms added on. It was a time of growth in every department.

The most significant growth came through the youth department. The youth group grew in great numbers under the leadership of Youth Pastors Jim and Robin Bolin, while director of the youth choir became my ministry. Together, we had a grand youth program, which was a model for many churches throughout the denomination.

Kelland's vision, enthusiasm, and love for people were evident throughout the Mableton Church. "Bro. Jeff" as he was affectionately called was actively engaged in the overall programs. All who heard him preach felt his compassion for the congregation. It was a great team for a great church!

The Mableton Youth Singers' fame spread throughout the region. They were State and National Champions in Teen Talent both 1976 and 1978. Each year we took a short tour in spring and fall, then an extended tour in the summer. The most memorable of all tours was to England in 1979.

Unfortunately, Kelland didn't get to go on tour to England with us. He got a blister on the ball of his left foot, which got infected and gave him much difficulty. But we had his blessings and prayers as we went to minister in the Elim Pentecostal Churches as well as the Church of God. We had marvelous services everywhere we went in London, Cheltenham, Birmingham, Stoke on Trent, Northampton, Stratford on Avon, Derby, to name a few. England's countryside is beautiful, but the sights in London were awesome, too.

The Mableton Youth Singers blessed the people and we were equally blessed by the churches we ministered to. We returned home to Mableton with memories to last a lifetime.

I was fortunate to have Danita and Keith on this tour. Danita was the lead soprano in the choir and Keith was the lead tenor. Also, Keith played trumpet with the Instrumental Ensemble. They were a great addition to the outstanding group of young singers and musicians. I thank God for every one of the forty young people who were a part of this memorable tour. I also appreciate the parents who served as chaperones and made financial sacrifices for their son or daughter to make the trip.

We were called upon to perform at civic affairs, State Capital, Lee College/University, Camp Meetings, revivals, Television appearances, and dozens of churches. It was a ministry! We saw many, many people fill the altars while the choir sang. And, to see the spiritual growth of the youth choir members themselves. Some received their call to ministry and are in full time ministry today.

Youth Pastors Jim and Robin Bolin felt the call to full-time ministry. We loved them dearly and hated to give them up. But, when God calls we relinquish our selfish wills and surrender to Him. We had enjoyed a phenomenal growth in the youth department, but the Bolins felt it was time to move on.

Jerry Rushing filled the vacancy as Youth Pastor. He, like Jim and Robin Bolin, was a choice servant of the Lord. He was a hard worker and soon found his place in the hearts of Mableton's youth. He blessed us with his melodious singing and wit.

Individual members of the youth choir developed and used their talents to the glory of God. Keith Jeffords, a *1978 National Teen Talent Winner in Brass Division,* used his excellence in trumpet by forming instrumental groups. He won many of his high school friends to the youth group through this effort. Also, he was key to getting a group together that won National Teen Talent that same year in the *Large Instrumental Ensemble Division*. These kids were a select group of talent.

Kelland's church office window faced the parking lot and back of the parsonage. He simply walked across the parking lot, entered the back door of the church to get to his office. It was convenient for him. Since he didn't drive his car to the church, one couldn't drive by and tell if he was in his office or not. Or, could they?

A yellow and white cat took up residence at our house and took a 'special' liking to Kelland. We don't know where she came from or whom she belonged to, but her favorite around our house was Kelland. When he left the house to go to the office, she followed him. As long as he was in the office, whether one hour or all day, the cat would patiently wait for him perched in his office window. When he left the office, the cat would hop down and leave with him.

It was hilarious! No matter how he tried to send her away, or trick her by going to the office another way, somehow she knew and would show up in his office window. Members would call or come by and say, "I see Bro. Jeff is in his office today. I saw the cat in the window."

Both Danita and Keith worked at Six Flags Over Georgia in the summer. It was a safe place to work and much fun. They came home everyday with stories to tell about their experiences of the day. It was always exciting for them to meet Church of God youth groups from throughout the southeast who came to enjoy a day of thrills at Six Flags Over Georgia. Six Flags was just a stone's throw from Mableton.

Kelland's began to have health problems toward the last of the Mableton pastorate. It had been six glorious years, but felt he should take a smaller church due to declining health. It was difficult to leave the good people of Mableton, but felt this was best for the church. Bro. Henson, State Overseer, understood his need and moved us to the Rainbow Drive Church, Decatur, Ga.

"If you are pleased with me, teach me your ways so I may know you and continue to find *favor* with you. Remember that this nation (church) is your people."

The Lord replied, "My presence will go with you, and I will give you rest." Exodus 33: 13-14

So too the (Holy) Spirit comes to our aid and bears us up in our weakness; for we do not know what prayer to offer nor how to offer it worthily as we ought, but the Spirit Himself goes to meet our supplication and pleads in our behalf with unspeakable yearnings and groanings too deep for utterance. Romans 8: 26

**Danita, Kelland, Nelia, Dianne and Keith
25th Wedding Anniversary**

Pastor Kelland Jeffords
Office - Mableton, GA

Mableton Youth Singers
Youth Night-General Assembly
National Teen Talent Winner – 1978

Mapleton Youth Singers
1978 National Teen Talent Champions
Robert Herrin - State Youth and Christian Education Director
Nelia Jeffords, Director

Mableton Youth Choir Director - Nelia Jeffords
General Youth and Christian Ed. Dir. Floyd Carey

Mableton Youth Singers - 1975
Georgia State Capitol
Atlanta, Georgia

National Teen Talent Winner
Large Instrumental Ensemble
Mableton, GA – 1978

Keith Jeffords -1978
National Teen Talent Winner
General Youth and Christian Ed. Dir.
Floyd Carey

Mableton Youth Singers
1976 National Teen Talent Champions

Pastor Jeffords & Jim Bolin

Keith, Nelia and Danita in England

1976 - Runner - Up
National Teen Talent
Small Instrumental Ensemble
David Gibson-Eddie Roach-Keith Jeffords

Kelland K. Jeffords

Nelia and Kelland Jeffords
Danita and Keith
Mabelton, GA - 1976

Pastor Jeffords - Jim Bolin

Keith Jeffords - Age 17 - Trumpet
1978 National Teen Talent Winner

Dianne Jeffords - Age 16 - Piano
1974 National Teen Talent winner

**Danita Jeffords-Florance
In Church**

Pastor Jim Bolin - Nelia Jeffords
1988

Sandra and Rodney Jeffords

Edgar and Aletha Waters – Nelia Jeffords

Kelland – Cape Cod, MA

Kelland and Nelia in New England

MEMORABLE TRIBUTES FROM FAMILY AND FRIENDS

TRINITY CHAPEL CHURCH OF GOD

JIM BOLIN, SENIOR PASTOR

Powder Springs, Georgia 30127

In the fall of 1974, God brought an incredible man and family into my life. Pastor Kelland Jeffords was to be an instrument of God to help me find my place in kingdom work. Little did I know that in just a few short months of his arrival as our new pastor that he would entrust me to lead the youth at the Mableton Church of God. Having virtually no experience but a willingness to learn, Pastor Jeffords took me under his wing and began to guide me toward my true calling, that of the pastor.

As I look back at those years, I realize just how much he impacted my life. Pastor Jeffords was a man of great compassion for hurting people. Often I watched him step in and help the "under-dog" achieve his or her goals. This was usually done without a lot of fanfare and a truly humble heart. His love was always open to people, yet he possessed a sense of discernment and wisdom that guided him and helped him to be firm when needed. Pastor Jeffords also demonstrated a sense of humor and honesty in the pulpit that disarmed most critics and became a conduit for the power of the Holy Spirit to flow through people.

There is one humorous experience that I must share that I will always remember. One night we were on a hospital visitation checking on one of the elderly women in our congregation. I was leaning on the passenger side door in his old trusted Ford Falcon when all of a sudden he took a quick left turn. Somehow the door flew open and out I went! I was barely hanging on and Pastor Jeffords, in his high-pitched squeal yelled, "Hang on Jim!" He reached across the car; (still going full steam ahead) grabbed me and helped me get back into the car. He saved my life that night, but I still laugh to this day when I think about what happened.

More than anything else, I want people to know Pastor Jeffords heart for God and the lost. He often laughed about not being the greatest preacher, but he knew his greatest gift was his ability to love people into the kingdom of God. He not only taught us the Word of God, but he showed us Jesus and that has been my model for years. There are a lot of great preachers and teachers, but few that consistently portray God and His love to this hurting world. Pastor Jeffords was that kind of pastor.

Kelland Jeffords passing was to say the least a sad day for me and my wife, Robin. His funeral was a mix of emotions, for we knew he was home, healed, and enjoying the presence of the Lord that he loved so much. To this day, we will always be thankful for Kelland and Nelia Jeffords influence on our lives and ministry.

Jim Bolin, Senior Pastor

"Ever Sense I Was a Puppy"

I first met Pastor Jeffords on a hot Georgia afternoon in August of 1974. The Church of God Generally Assembly had just completed, and word was sent by church members who had attended that Kelland K. Jeffords had been appointed as pastor of our church. I knew of Brother Jeffords and his family for he was just completing an assignment as the Church of God State Youth and Christian Education Director for Georgia. I had never met him, and like everyone else, was anxious for his arrival.

I remember there was a sense of excitement that permeated the gathering that day as many of gathered to welcome the new pastor and his family to town. We began to look to the future and what God would do in our church. I think I was more excited about the fact that he had a son close to my age who wanted to be a part of band at the high school I attended. I knew this would give us something in common and that offered a potential for a new friend.

Little did I know at the time the impact that 'this' pastor would have on me and the future course of my life. I remember one the first times I talked at length with Pastor Jeffords, we were discussing how long he had been in the ministry. Always the teacher and a master at using humor to make a point, he launched into telling me a story about a man who went to see a psychiatrist. The man told the doctor, "I feel like a dog." The doctor then asked him, "How long have you felt like a dog?" To which to man replied, "Ever sense I was a puppy." I remember thinking, this guy is crazy, but the seemingly lightheartedness and lack of stuffiness was appealing and refreshing to see in a pastor. I soon learned that telling stories and using humor were a big part of his teaching style and a major way he dealt with people. I was just the latest to experience this technique.

He went on to tell me that he had to some extent felt the calling of God upon his life from his early years of growing up in rural South Georgia. While he often wandered what that calling would look like in the future, he never doubted that God had a work for him to do. This one conversation impacted my life and future in a tremendous way, and became the foundation for many conversations that helped me to: broaden and refine my scope and understanding of ministry; grasp the nature, mystery, and ministry of the Church; explore the true meaning of worship and the implications of its expression whether in exuberant or reserved manner.

Pastor Jeffords was a man of integrity and compassion, always looking for ways to bring out the best in a person. The thing that set him a part was his contagious ability to believe in people. He was a people-centered pastor, you always knew that he 'was for you.' I saw him stick with individuals when the human side of myself was screaming to cut them loose and cut your losses. But he was the consummate pastor, always ministering with the motivation of a shepherd, willing to leaving the ninety-nine to find the one.

As the years went by, I got to know him at a deeper level. I found him to be solidly grounded in the Word of God. He unapologetically believed that the Gospel of Jesus Christ was the gospel unto salvation and passionately proclaimed it. He understood that the Gospel could change people's lives and he was not ashamed of it.

He fervently proclaimed the Gospel with the conviction that it touches the lives of individuals at precisely those points which are the same for every human, regardless of their cultural or social milieu. Loneliness, guilt, lack of purpose, insecurity, inner turmoil, fear of death, anxiety, incompleteness, frustration and boredom are but a few of the universal human experiences to which he believed Jesus could change.

He believed further that the Gospel offers not only a dynamic solution, but also a radical cure for the mortal disease of which these problems were simply symptoms. He often quoted the Apostle Paul, "Therefore if any man be in Christ, he is a new creature: old things are passed away; behold, all things are become new" (II Cor. 5:17).

This was reflected in those who attended the Mableton Church of God. During his tenure as pastor, for the first time we saw African Americans, Latinos, Asians, the rich and poor begin attending the church, becoming a family, and integrating themselves into the church's programs and ministry. Everyone was welcomed; no one was shunned or rejected. For Pastor Jeffords, the foot of the Cross was truly level and there was room for all.

Pastor Jeffords was often considered to be ahead of his time in his understanding of and approach to church growth and Christian Education. His insights and leadership resulted in the Mableton Church of God growing to experience its largest Sunday School and Morning Worship attendance. All departments flourished under his ministry. Much of this can be attributed to his ministry philosophy of seeing himself as not only the pastor of a local church, but the pastor of the local community. His ministry impacted the local schools, the nursing homes, the police departments, and a multitude of other organizations outside of the Mableton Church of God congregation.

It was during the summer of 1998 that Pastor Jeffords had his greatest impact on my life. I had enrolled at Lee College and felt God leading me into the ministry. As my pastor, I sought his counsel. After listening to me, he said, "David, how sure are you that God has called you to be a minister of the Gospel?" I was caught off guard, and said, "I'm trying to figure this out Pastor. I'm really not sure." His reply hit me like an arrow straight to my heart. He said, "David, if you can do anything else besides being in the ministry, and be satisfied, then do it. But if you can't get away from that pull to ministry, and will never be satisfied doing something else, then preach the Gospel in the power of the Holy Spirit."

Many times I have measured and evaluated my ministry in light of those gentle and wisdom packed words. In those times when I have been discouraged with ministry and dealing with people, I hear Pastor Jeffords words ringing in my ears, "David, can you do anything else and be satisfied?" Time and time again I come back to a resounding NO!

By his life and illustration, Pastor Jeffords gave me an example of what it meant to be a Minister of the Gospel. He lived before me not only the joys and victories of being a pastor, but its frustrations and heartbreaks as well. He was not merely my pastor; he was my friend.

I am a better, Christian, minister, and military chaplain because of him. If I had to sum up his ministry, for him it was all about the relationships he nurtured and then sent out. At the end of the day, his legacy will not be about the buildings or programs that were left behind. The thing that will continue to distinguish him is that his ministry will keep on living through the lives of so many who under his ministry were called, trained and sent forth as ministers of the Gospel. I am fortunate in being one of them.

David L. Gibson
Commander, U.S. Navy Chaplain Corps

CAN YOU AND I CHANGE THE WORLD?

I just wasn't used to a Church of God service. I was attending the First Church of the Frigidare. You know? Where the Lord's frozen chosen came every Sunday. I learned early that "wild fire" was better than "no fire", so I made the move.

I went with my family to First Baptist Church in Mableton, Georgia on Sunday mornings and to the wild fire church on Sunday evenings. Brother Jeffords, as I affectionately called him, said I was a Bapticostal! That didn't last long though. That teenage boy soon became a full-fledged, blood bought, born-again, devil stomping, tongues talking Church of God Pentecostal, which just about scared my family to death.

It was not until my dad was in the hospital to have some kidney stones removed that he started warming up to the fire. Brother Jeffords paid my dad a visit in the hospital. Immediately after that visit, I felt no pressure from my dad or family about attending the Mableton Church of God at any time. It is amazing what a smile can do. A few kind words. An earnest prayer. A gentle touch. This is what happened when Brother Jeffords entered the hospital to see my dad and that 'man of God' never changed.

My dad did change. Even though he still attends the Baptist church, he sneaks off to get warmed up at the various Church of Gods his kids and grandkids now attend. And there is no reluctance or hesitation when he walks through a Church of God door because a loving Church of God pastor brought a pleasant conversation, an earnest prayer, and a gentle touch when he needed it most.

Of course this opened up doors for me. Now, I could go to the Church of God freely, I freely received. I freely received a true separation from the world-salvation. I freely received the baptism of the Holy Ghost. I freely received a calling from God to tell others what Christ had done for me. All this was because God had sent an anointed pastor and family to the Mableton community at the Mableton Church of God.

It never ceased to amaze me how Brother Jeffords effortlessly lived and spoke about Christ the Lord. Here I was, as a young man, struggling with peer pressure and a young minister struggling to verbalize what Christ had done for me. It came so easy for Brother Jeffords.

Brother Jeffords invited me to attend the South Georgia Campmeeting with him, so I jumped in the car, and we headed off. Down a long rural road Brother Jeffords sees an old country store and says, "Tim, let's go in and get us a RC Cola and moon pie." So, I agreed even though I got a coke and a pack of crackers. I stood at the counter with him as we drank our drinks and snacks. He looked outside and back to the man behind the counter and said, "It's a beautiful day, isn't it?" "Yep," was the man's reply. "It's a beautiful day for the Lord Jesus to come back. Are you ready?" asked Brother Jeffords.

Then I saw the man behind the counter encounter the Lord. Tears rolling down his cheeks and he said, "I'm away from God but surely He sent you my way today." I stood there and watched a man flowing with ease, the spirit of God leading him and speaking life through him. Brother Jeffords reached for the man's hand, they knelt behind the counter and I heard that man's prayer as he came back to God.

Can you and I change the world? I think so. How? Like Brother Jeffords – one man at a time. No matter where we are and what we do - the lesson I learned from Brother Jeffords that day is to live the Christian life and the urgency of Christ's return. Don't be afraid to share your faith, to smile when you order a RC Cola and moon pie – the person behind the counter may need it to make it back home.

Tim Trotter

Me and Kelland:
A Memorable Testimony
Bob L. Johnson, Jr.

He was a great guy and he was from Waresboro. He was sort of proud of that and quite pleased to tell folks that he had gone to school with Pernell Roberts (a.k.a Adam Cartright of *Bonanza* fame).

He was also warm and funny. Not necessarily in the jokes he told, but in his style and demeanor. Kelland loved his family and he loved young people.

My initial introduction to the Jeffords family was during my undergraduate days at Lee. It wasn't Kelland, Sr. that I first met; it was Keith and his mom, Nelia. I was sitting in a practice room on the second floor of the old music building near Hughes Hall. Frustrated, yet working diligently to master the etude before me, I was interrupted by a knock at the door. Before I could drop the horn from my lips, a stocky outgoing young man opened the door, extended his hand and exclaimed, "Hi! I'm Keith! That sounded pretty good.... I'm a trumpet player too, and I'll be at Lee next year."

That was in the fall 1976 or spring of 77 - I can't remember - but it was *my* introduction to the Jeffords family. Keith and I would eventually become fast friends. Little did I then know that our career ambitions and love of music would soon bind us together as brothers. These commonalities would later serve as points of departure for many animated discussions. Our discussions covered a wide-range of serious, humorous, and at times bizarre topics: our educational aspirations; the Church of God; great music; bad music; great and bad music in the Church of God; Teen Talent; fun times at youth camp; the richness, frustrations, and at times odd experiences of growing up Pentecostal.and other such things. I think he was surprised to come to Lee and find a student who go toe-to-toe with him discussing the great Russian masters - Tchaikovsky, Borodin and Smetna - all the while equally at ease with the music of Charles B. Wycuffe, C.S. Grogan, Charles Towler, the latest Convention Book out of Pathway, and the Red Back Hymnal. Upon cue, both of us – without any music whatsoever – could launch into singing an array of Convention- and Hymn- Book selections we had grown up hearing. We made it a game to see who could remember the words, specific book, and page numbers of each. We were all too eager to strain (or should I say *bust*) our vocal-chords in a comedic effort to wail the alto lines made famous by so many. It was quite the challenge for our male voices!

Neither of us had encountered many people in our worlds who could talk with ease and humor about these contrasting musical experiences. But we could and we did. I had large LP collection that Keith both loved and envied. With the old Lee Singers albums or Moody Chorale playing in he background, we spent hours listening, talking, singing and laughing till our sides hurt. It was heady stuff for both of us and we drew inspiration from it. To this day, I fondly remember the solemn moments we experienced listening to the great choral arrangements of *I Will Sing of My Redeemer*, *My Eternal King* and *A Mighty Fortress*. They moved our emotions and evoked praise at a deep level back then. They still do. Such experiences defined our early friendship. Though now living 2,000 miles apart and frustrated by the challenges this brings, they continue to bind us. That was 30 years ago. Today, when we have the occasion to talk on the phone or meet in person, we pick up right where we left off. You know, life is sort of blessed and funny that way. Reunions with friends such as this represent *oasis-moments* in life. I'm convinced they offer us a taste of heaven.

This is how I came to know the Jeffords family: through Keith and experiences together at Lee. Yet this reflection is neither about Keith nor me. It's about Keith's parents, particularly his father, Kelland, Sr. But then, you really can't talk about Kelland without talking about his family, his kids - Diane, Keith and Danita - and his awesome life-partner, Nelia Flowers. They provide the context for understanding *who* he was and *why he meant so much* to so many. You certainly can't reflect on Kelland without thinking about Nelia. They were partners in ministry. The ministry gifts and successes experienced by each were expressions of their faithfulness and labor of love together. They were a team.

I would eventually get to know Kelland, Sr. a couple of years later while living for a time in Atlanta. Recently graduated from Lee, I had moved there and enrolled in graduate school at Emory. Having a difficult time finding a place to live, the Jeffords invited me to stay with them until I could get to know the place and feel more at ease. It was a tough time for me and I quickly discovered that I wasn't ready for it.

The move to Atlanta led to the convergence of several conflicting emotions. I was struggling with the transition from college to life. I had just left the comfortable, nurturing confines of Lee where I had spent four years growing, pursuing my call, and having the time of my life. Lee was great fun for me and it was a safe environment. Now I was "out there" on my on, living in a huge city, enrolled at a large imposing, secular university and overwhelmed. In addition, I found myself *really* living away from Mom and Dad and all the securities this afforded. With the move to Atlanta, I had experienced this as a sense of loss. Granted, it was only 250 miles from Oak Ridge, but for a kid who was still fairly connected with the comforts of home, this too was a change for which I was unprepared (*don't laugh*). While at Lee, I enjoyed the luxury of jumping in the car and going home at a moments notice. Psychologically, I was both *away from* home, yet still *at* home. The move to an area where I had no friends and only a handful of acquaintances was a drastic change.

In addition, I was love sick in a bad kind of way with a girl back at Lee. I had just broken up with my soon-to-be wife and the prospects of getting back together were from my perspective *nil*. I was in the process of moving on with life. In my mind I had done this, but emotionally I continued to struggle. All these things converged within me once in Atlanta. This is the mindset and these are the circumstances under which I came to know Kelland and Nelia.

No doubt, their impressions of me during these years must have lead them to conclude that I was one strange kid whose career aspirations would soon be trumped by his emotional hang-ups and baggage. Yet they welcomed me into their home, gave me a place to stay and fed my many meals (*everyone knows that all the Flowers sisters can cook!*). Reflecting on the short time I lived with them, there are few things that stand out in my mind that define and exemplify who Kelland Jeffords was. Allow me to share these impressions below in and around a handful of short anecdotes.

Kelland loved and invested in the lives of young people. While I didn't grow up in Georgia and experience his leadership at the state level, one thing I quickly picked up on was that he and Nelia loved teenagers. This love led them to wisely invest in the lives of countless numbers of kids in unusual ways. I learned this shortly after moving in with them. Both were quite gracious in their hospitality and acceptance of me *and* the host of other kids who had come before me. After a few weeks, I was surprised to learn the names and number of young people in the Church who had lived with them at various points in time. I was one of many to be taken in by them and loved as their own. They were generous and gracious. In thinking about Kelland almost 20 years after his promotion, it is this spirit of acceptance and hospitality that defines for me who Kelland and Nelia were. I was extended the same hospitality and encouragement that many other kids had received from them. I will always remember Kelland and Nelia for this. While they may not understand the great impact of this influence during my short stay with them, I am thankful to them for it. It's indicative of how actions speak louder than words and exemplifies Biblical hospitality: *A bishop must be...given to hospitality* - **I Timothy 3:2.**

I was equally surprised to see the number and vitality of kids that seemed to flock around the Jeffords at the Mableton Church of God. Again, I was soon to discover that this had defined the Jeffords ministry for years. Together they had built an incredibly talented and energized youth group. Though I had been a part of two great youth choirs in my younger days in Tennessee and had enjoyed great times of fellowship, the youth group at Mableton was the most energized, talented and ambitious group of kids I had ever seen in *one* church. I'm not talking about North Cleveland, Westmore or Mt Paran, I'm talking about the Mableton Church of God. They loved each other; they loved to sing; and they loved the

Jeffords! With kids coming and going, laughing and enjoying
fellowship in a way only teenagers can do, there were moments
when the parsonage felt like Grand Central Station. It was an
amazing thing to witness! Though I'm sure this at times encroached
on their private lives, Kelland and Nelia welcomed it.

As a minister's son, I could appreciate the effort that went
into building the youth group. As a musician, I also appreciated
what it took to channel the energy of these kids into a choir that sang
with anointing and skill. Nelia took the lead with the choir, but
Kelland was always there encouraging. I was impressed with his
love of music and the way he supported Nelia in using her ministry
gifts. I was also struck by what the kids did for Kelland and Nelia,
how their singing, excitement and presence invigorated them. They
were energized by the kids. It was a great time and wonderful
match for the Jeffords and the Mableton Church of God. The choir
became national Teen Talent winners on two different occasions.
As a result of the Jeffords' love of music and willingness to invest in
people, many of these kids' lives were changed forever. Kelland's
example reminds me of the importance of music to life and the
transforming power it can have when used as a tool of ministry: *sing
and make melody in your hearts to the Lord* - **Ephesians 5:19b**.

A third anecdote sheds further light on the kind of man
Kelland was. My Dad had given me an off-white, eight-cylinder,
1966 Chevrolet Impala to take to graduate school. It certainly
wasn't a babe magnet, but I was student-poor and it was wheels!
Grateful for this and his willingness to pay for the insurance, I
commanded it with a modicum of genuine albeit youthful pride.

Having been in Atlanta for several days, I decided to head to
a mall on the northeastern side of town. It was late afternoon.
Thirty years later I can't remember exactly why I was going, but
onward I went. Those who live in the Atlanta know how hectic
traffic can be, particularly when navigating from one side of town to
the other. While driving north at 65 mph on Interstate 75 past Mt.
Paran Road just a mile or two south of the I-75-285 interchange, I
heard a loud pop a felt a rather hard jolt to the car. Panic stricken, I
quickly found myself grasping the wheel of my vehicle trying to

control it as it skidded at a titled-angle down the interstate on three wheels and a nub. The right front wheel of my car had broken off! Traffic was heavy and cars were flying by. As the adrenaline flowed, I glanced up to see the broken wheel of my car – tire undamaged – bouncing down the interstate at a high rate of speed like a basketball. It jumped *over* the concrete barrier dividing north- from southbound lanes careening into oncoming traffic. I could see southbound drivers frantically swerving to avoid it.

After what seemed like an eternity, my 66 Impala finally came to a stop on the side of the road. When it did, I took a deep breath, let out a "Thank You, Jesus!" and got out of my car to survey the damage. Needless to say, I had a problem! Somewhat hypnotized by the trauma of the moment, I briefly forgot about the broken wheel that had danced down the road in front of me into oncoming traffic. Regaining presence-of-mind, I carefully navigated my way across several lanes of traffic to survey the damage it had caused to other vehicles. Thankfully, it too had come to a stop without hitting a single car. Unharmed, feeling my heart pound like a drum in my chest, and looking down to check my paints, I breathed another sigh of relief thanking God again for His protection.

By now, you the reader obviously know *who* God sent to help me through the challenges of that day. Yes, it was Kelland. I called and informed him of my circumstances. Brother Jeffords immediately went into action. It just so happened that the Newtons, members of the Mableton congregation owned a service station a few miles north on I-75. Kelland called him. A tow truck was soon dispatched. By the end of the day, I had been shuttled safely back to the Jeffords home. It took a couple of weeks to get my vehicle repaired.

Not many folks know about this story. Those who do have probably forgotten it. Fewer still know that he loaned me his old faded VW Beetle to go back-and-forth to school until my car was fixed (*Some of us remember Kelland's other "famous" cars. Remember the Ford Falcon?*). I never paid him for using it and he never asked. Even if he had, I didn't have the money. I felt bad about this. Not only was I boarding at his house and eating at his table, I was now *driving* one of his cars. All the while, Kelland encouraged and continued to welcome me. Kelland was both kind and giving. For this, I am thankful. It personified his attitude and willingness to give, help, and encourage many young people like me: *for God loves a cheerful giver* – **2 Corinthians 9:7b**.

The final story I share about Kelland is perhaps my favorite. In many ways, it exemplifies how parents hope and pray the best for their children and how these hopes play out in subsequent generations. Little did I know that the experiences Kelland was going through with his son Keith in the late 1970s, I would be going through with my own son BJ some 30 years later.

Kelland loved his kids, each of them dearly. Of the three, I was closest to Keith. Keith had always had dreams of becoming a doctor. He had shared this with me on many occasions and all our mutual friends knew it. He was passionate about it. Even in the early days of our friendship, it was obvious to me that this was his calling.

While I was living with the Jeffords in Atlanta, Keith was still a pre-med major at Lee working hard to position himself for med school under the dutiful, disciplined eye of that infamous yet loving taskmaster Lois Beach. Needless to say, his parents were both supportive and excited for him. However, they were well aware of the competitiveness of the admissions process. It has been said that the hardest, most nerve-racking part of medical school is getting in. Having had friends and now a son experience this process, I can understand this statement. It's a tedious, prolonged and at times expensive process filled with emotional highs and lows.

I can't tell you the number of times Kelland, Sr. would ask me, "*Brother Bobby, do you think Keith will get into med school?*

Brother Bobby, do you really think Keith will get into med school?" Even as I write these words, I can still hear the inflection of his high-pitched voice as we sat together early one afternoon at the counter of a local Mableton diner enjoying doughnuts together,"*Brother Bobby, do you think Keith will get into med school?*" Given his diabetic condition, Kelland wasn't suppose to be eating sweets like this.   But that particular day without Nelia's knowledge or permission, we had hustled off to the doughnut shop to enjoy this small yet forbidden American culinary pleasure together.

I never grew tired of Kelland asking this question. I knew Keith well by then and was quite confident that he would eventually realize his dreams. Though Keith would humorously needle his dad for hours on end about this perpetual questioning, I knew Kelland's motives behind it. He loved Keith. It was obvious to me that sooner or later – somehow, someway, somewhere – Keith would get accepted. My answer to Kelland's question was as honest as his motive for asking.

Kelland didn't live to see Keith graduate with his DDS from Emory or MD Eastern Virginia. Neither did he see his son receive the Brittain Award as he walked across the stage that inviting spring day in Atlanta. *"Yes, Brother Jeffords, like I assured you back then that day in Mableton at the doughnut shop, Keith got into to medical school and you would be proud of him!"*

Little did I know then that I would go through the same medical school *angst* with my son BJ some 30 years later. Little did I also know that it would be Kelland's son who would play a significant role in BJ's life as encourager and cheerleader.   I understood Kelland's line of questioning then, but I think I understand it even better now: *faithful is He who calls you, who also will do it* **– I Thessalonians 5:24**.

It was a sad day for me and my brother Ben when word came that Kelland had passed. We both loved him. He and Nelia were pastoring the Rainbow Church of God in Decatur. By that time all three of his kids had left the nest. I was living in Baton Rouge finishing my degree at LSU. Carol and I had been married for about seven years and were enjoying our son BJ and newborn Katie.

I desperately wanted to go the funeral. I loved Kelland, Nelia and Keith. I owed it the entire family. Yet the scheduling of the service was such that I didn't have time to drive from Baton Rouge to Atlanta. There was also no money available for me to catch a flight. We were living on a meager, part-time church salary and graduate stipend. It took all we made to live. Beyond that we had no money for "extras." Carol, however, insisted that I go. I don't remember exactly how we came up with the money for the last-minute flight, but we did. Somehow God provided and I went. I'm glad I did. The funeral home and church were packed. Keith, Diane and Danita sang *Til the Storm Passes By*. It was a great tribute and promotion service for Kelland: ***precious in the sight of the LORD is the death of His saints* – Psalm 116:15.**

My wonderful Mormon friends talk to me on occasion about how important it is for the faithful to continually "bear witness to their testimony." As a son of Pentecost, I think I know what they mean. Such talk is nothing new to the rich tradition that has historically defined our Church. Our testimonies spring from a biblically rooted, Spirit-empowered faith that gives every believer a unique identity and witness. Contemplating the life-testimonies of those saints who have since joined the "cloud of witnesses" cheering us onward, we are encouraged to remain steadfast in our own commitments and testify to His work in our lives.

Now nineteen years removed from his death, this is how I choose to remember Kelland. His testimony continues to speak. For those of us who knew and loved him, it is a *hallowed* testimony. He was loving. He was generous in his giving. He was an encourager who wisely chose to invest in the lives of hundreds of young people. During the 1970s and 80s, I was one of those kids. His testimony has now become a part of our testimonies....*my* testimony: ***I thank my God on every remembrance of you* – Philippians 4:3a**.

About the author

Bob L. Johnson, Jr is a long-time family friend of the Jeffords. He and his wife Carol have lived for years in Bountiful, Utah, a suburb of Salt Lake City. They are the proud parents of two children: BJ and Katie Marie. He is a professor of educational leadership and policy at the University of Utah and an ordained minister in the Church of God. His current call as a policy analyst is to help society address the opportunities and challenges that public and higher education.

Chapter 10

The Final Move

Keith had graduated from Lee College (now Lee University) with honors. He had applied to a number of universities for his post graduate studies in medicine. Kelland would faithfully walk to the mailbox each day to see if his acceptance letter was in the mail. The waiting was over when he was accepted to Emory University School of Dentistry in Atlanta, Georgia.

Danita lived with Charles and Datha Darby in Mableton, Georgia during her senior year at Pebblebrook High School. We moved to Decatur, Georgia to pastor the Rainbow Church of God. Danita came home every weekend. It just made good sense for her to stay behind and finish high school with her friends, and she was so involved with musical activities at Pebblebrook High and that mandated it. It was a sacrifice for Danita. We are eternally grateful to Charles and Datha for their benevolence. They are good people. Thank you for your gracious hospitality.

Danita and Keith were a blessing to us as their parents. They both worked diligently in the Rainbow Church and at home. They used their talents to assist where needed. For this we were grateful. Thank you, Danita and Keith, for making our load a little lighter.

Danita enrolled at DeKalb State University (a division of the University of Georgia) following graduation. She later decided to attend Lee College where she could further use and expand her musical talents. She was privileged to sing with the renowned *Lee Singers,* under the direction of Jim Burns. She made many friends, enjoyed Lee College, but love won out!

She didn't return to Lee because she and fiancé, Bob Florance, planned a March wedding at Mountain West Church of God in Tucker, Georgia. It was an extraordinary event. *Lee Singers and Jim Burns* sang for the memorable affair. It was beautiful in every

way. After a honeymoon to the island of St. Martin, they moved to
Boston, Massachusetts. Bob was employed by Data General
Corporation.

After arriving in Boston, Danita soon enrolled at Worchester State
University to continue her studies. Bob received another promotion
with a move to Minneapolis, Minnesota. Again, Danita transferred
to the University of Minnesota, and completed her Bachelor of
Science degree in Business. Eventually, they transferred to Atlanta,
Georgia and have remained for good. Bob, later had a career change
and is now employed by Oracle.

We gave the church our best. But, our best wasn't what it used to be.
In spite of Kelland's limitations, the church moved forward in all
departments. We were grateful for those that became his helpers.
Kelland's eyesight had failed and could no longer drive. The Lord
provided a faithful brother in the church, Luther Nance, who drove
the car for him. He took him to make hospital visits, shut-ins, or
wherever he needed to go.

Many times he would cry and say to me, "You know if I could visit
like I use to, the church would be filled." My heart hurt with him.
He had to listen to tapes for Bible reading and to prepare his
sermons. He would then tell me what to write and I would write out
his sermons with a black felt tip pen in big letters. He could see a
little, but the hemorrhages in the back of his eyes left them so
damaged. Even with laser to stop the bleeding it wouldn't correct
what eyesight had been lost. The doctor's declared him 'legally
blind.'

One year he was in the hospital five times. I had launched a late
career with Bristol-Myers Squibb. I knew that I would eventually
have to become the breadwinner. His health was declining so fast.
He was happy when I got a promotion and thankful for the
opportunity the Lord had given me. He realized disability
retirement was inevitable.

My mother was a charter member of Blanton's Grove Church of
God and a day was set aside to honor her many years of faithfulness

in April 1986. Kelland was one of several speakers for that occasion. While there we were, we visited my sister and brother-in-law, Virginia and Darius Floyd. During the visit, Virginia asked Kelland the question, "Kelland if you had your life to live over, is there anything differently that you would do?" Kelland thought for a minute and said, "if I could do anything differently, I would spend more time with my children."

No regrets for him and life's work for God. Perhaps, only a little more time with his children. They grow up so fast. Before you realize they are off to college, married, and having a family of their own. Do we get the message?

During the pastorate at Rainbow Drive Church of God in Decatur, Georgia (1980-1987) my career with Bristol-Myers Squibb Company had gone from part-time to full-time as a Sales Representative. God was directing my career. I didn't realize it at the time. But, as I look back I can see how he directed every step.

Kelland was so supportive and encouraging. When I met my sales goals, he rejoiced with me. Sometimes I would have to leave home very early in the morning. He would be waiting at the carport door to check me if I had my sales bag, car keys, coat, hand bag, money for lunch, and the list goes on. He knew I would be in a distant city and would need these things. Oh, how I became dependent on him. He thought for me. As I left for the day he would say, "I'll be praying for a safe trip."

My mother had come for a visit. I was working and left her with Kelland. When I came home that evening, Kelland was laughing and filled me in with the happenings of the day. He was going to make a call and ask mother to go with him. She said, "Kelland I can't find my pocketbook. Can you help me find it?" She and Kelland looked all over the house and could not find the pocketbook. They searched. They looked. Finally, Kelland said, "Ma, can't you go without it? We'll look again when we get back." So, out the door they started. Just then Kelland saw that the missing pocketbook was on her arm. Both had a jolly good laugh over that episode.

The grandchildren were company for him. Dianne worked two and three jobs to reach her financial needs. Having gone through a very painful divorce, she was given custody of her four boys and it took all of us helping out. Rather than leave the boys home alone, Grandmother and Granddaddy's Jeffords house became their second home; especially during summertime when school was out. Many quality hours were spent with the boys and their granddaddy.

Michael (age 13), Eric and Derek (twins, age 11), and Matthew (age 6) were a lively sort. They were boys! The time spent with 'granddaddy' was invaluable. I had re-entered college at DeKalb Community College in order to enhance my career. When I graduated, the grandsons were there. When I walked across the stage after receiving my diploma, Michael was there waiting to give me a big hug and said, *"Grandmother, I'm one proud grandson"*.

I woke early one February morning in 1987 and started planning Kelland's retirement celebration. I shared the details with Kelland and Keith. They liked them. I knew who would do exactly what at his retirement party. He had an illustrious thirty-seven years of ministry and I wanted him to receive the honor he deserved. He was making plans to retire in June of that same year.

In late March, he wanted to go see his mother who had just gotten out of the hospital. I took several days off from work and drove him to Waresboro. While there he became faint and weak. I thought it was the warm weather making him react this way. We decided it better to get him back home in Decatur where he would be in an air-conditioned house.

Again, Sunday in morning worship service he had a weak spell while in the pulpit. Keith came immediately to assist his father to a chair. After church, I drove him to the hospital and had the emergency room doctor check him out. He sent us home, as he found no reason to keep him there. Monday morning I made an appointment for him to see his primary care physician. They set his appointment for Wednesday.

In the meantime I got a call from the Bristol-Myers Squibb regional office that the Regional Director wanted to see me and that I should be there by 1:00 PM. When I got to the office, the Eastern Division and Regional Directors told me that I had been promoted to District Sales Representative. I called Kelland and told him the exciting news. He was struggling for breath but managed to say, "Congratulations Nelia, now we won't have to worry about finances when I retire."

On Wednesday, he went for his doctor's appointment. He sent him immediately to Georgia Baptist Hospital. His condition went from bad to worse. He suffered a stroke on early Friday morning. Dr. Ford assured me with therapy he would be able to regain his mobility. I was cautiously optimistic. But, early on the following Monday morning Dr. Ford called to say he had suffered a massive stroke sometime during the night and explained his condition. I knew this wasn't good. I called the children. Danita and Bob lived in Minneapolis, Minnesota and were on the first plane to Atlanta. Keith was somewhere on Emory University Campus. Dianne was getting ready for work. I rushed to the hospital. Keith and Dianne came right away. Danita got to Atlanta later that morning.

I was praying with him, and as we prayed he lifted his right hand in praise to the Lord. His left side paralyzed and unable to speak, doctor's rushed him to intensive care. His conditioned worsened. Everything went wrong that could go wrong. The children and I stood vigil by his bedside singing songs, reading scripture, praying for a miracle. We surrendered our will to God's will. He slipped into a coma and after several days on life support went home to be with the Lord. What a comfort to the family to know the last communication we had with him was 'praising his Lord.'

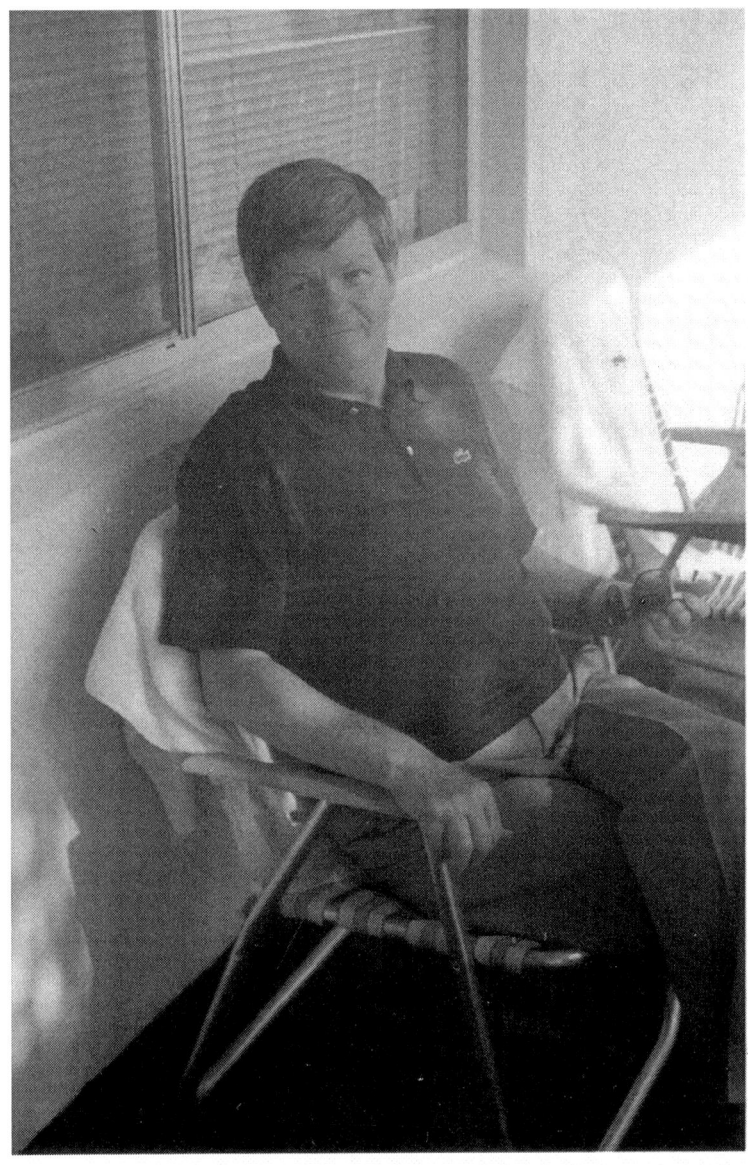

Kelland Jeffords Relaxing

David McBrayer – Kelland Jeffords

Benny and Sharon Priest
Little Kelland Priest

Raymond Jeffords and Keith Jeffords
Waycross, Georgia

Dianne and four boys
Michael, Derek, Eric, Matthew

Nelia and Kelland 1983

Nelia and Kelland in 1985

Nelia's Graduation, DeKalb State University

Danita and Bob's Wedding with Jeffords Family

Chapter 11

The Coronation

In February 1987, I was confident the Lord had spoken to me about his retirement service but, it wasn't his retirement. Instead, it was the celebration of his home-going!

At the viewing in Decatur on Thursday evening, April 23, 1987, hundreds and hundreds gathered to pay their respects. People came from far and near because they loved the man Kelland Jeffords. The floral display spread into room after room of the funeral home. It was an outpouring of love as people came because they cared and wanted to say "thanks" to a man who had given his life so unselfishly caring for others.

His Coronation Service was celebrated on Friday, April 24, 1987 at Rainbow Church of God, Decatur, Ga., under the direction of our longtime friend and fellow-minister, Rev. Paul H. Henson. Several ministers gave tribute to the dynamic ministry of a man who ultimately had given his life willingly to advance the kingdom of God. Literally hundreds and hundreds of people filled the church to overflowing. We laughed, we cried, and, we rejoiced as each one recalled an event, or happening, that was shared with him during his lifetime. The funeral service lasted more than two hours but it didn't seem that long. The beautiful singing included his favorite songs both congregational and by 'special' rendition. Truly, it was a celebration of his life's ministry.

David McBrayer was one of the many hundreds in attendance that day. He had terminal cancer and was given only a short time to live. David had been so considerate to drive Kelland to and from state church functions before both their health conditions worsened. Kelland had made the statement to me, "I don't know what I'll do when David is gone." He really expected David to go first. David died nine days following Kelland's death. I think their relationship could be akin to Jonathan and David in the Bible. David was pastor of the Milford Church of God.

In his book, *Language of Love*, Dr. Robert E. Fisher wrote on pages 134-135 his thoughts while helping with Kelland's funeral. He served as State Overseer of North Georgia at the time and was favorably impressed with comments by fellow minister's who had known Kelland through the years.

"Honest words of appreciation and a lack of criticism are not only edifying to the person spoken about, but also to those who observe and hear. Recently, I was involved in the funeral of a pastor who was known for his skill in telling stories. *Kelland Jeffords* could keep an audience (from one to hundreds) spellbound as he recounted in intimate detail, often with a humorous touch, the behavior of people he knew. He loved people and had a special insight into how they behaved.

The most significant thing to me about Kelland's skill in storytelling was his ability to illustrate colorfully the uniqueness of human nature without ever being critical or poking fun. When he finished telling a story about a person, you felt good about that person and better about yourself. The outpouring of *love and appreciation* at his funeral (was termed a coronation) was strong testimony to the edifying way he related to and talked about others".

Keith and Nelia
State Overseer - Robert E. Fisher - 1987

At the request of his beloved friend Grady Maxwell, Jr., owner of Westwood Gardens Funeral Home in Griffin, Ga., his body was taken to Griffin for viewing on Friday night. It had been twenty-one years since we left the pastorate in Griffin. Yet, hundreds and hundreds of friends paid their respects to a man whom they loved unconditionally. That mutual love still continues today.

Interment Service was held the next day on Saturday, April 25, at Pinecrest Memorial Gardens in Jesup, Georgia with Rev. J. Edgar Waters and Rev. Bruce Flowers officiating. The drive from Decatur to Jesup was somber and rather lengthy. Our saddened spirits were uplifted to see hundreds of family members and friends waiting at the cemetery to say goodbye to one so well loved.

A short service was held at the graveside in final tribute. It was a majestic ceremony. Joyful songs rang out as voices blended together in melodious tones sang about God's unfailing love. Comforting prayers for the family made the sacredness of the hour awe-inspiring. As we said good-bye to our precious loved one we left with hope in our hearts. We shall see him again!

One of Kelland's most favorite songs that gave him inspiration to go about his daily routine when he felt otherwise was *"I'll Never Pass This Way Again"*. Written by Ronnie Gaylord, it speaks volumes to the individual as to the reality of life....we only pass this way but once. Whatever we do we must do it now because we will never pass this way again.

Yesterday is gone. We do not have the promise of tomorrow. Today is the opportunity that God has given us to do all the good that we possibly can. The kindness, the love we give, must be done now for we'll never pass this way again.

He was only fifty-eight years old and too young to die. He had so much more to give, I thought. The disease of diabetes has no mercy on the young or old. It finally took his life, *but his effervescent spirit lives on.*

On his grave marker reads: *"...... he served his generation by the will of God , and fell asleep......"* Acts 13:36a

Bronze Blanket Grave Cover

Songwriter Audrey Mieir wrote the song, *"It Matters To Him"*. This song became a favorite because it applies to us as an individual. It gives the picture of a big loving God who has time to see about our personal needs. Although He has the sun, the moon, the stars, and millions of souls to see about, He's just as close and can be reached by a whispered prayer. He is busy but not too busy to care about our heartaches, our sorrows, or whatever our needs. It does "Matter To Him About You".

"I have fought a good fight, I have finished my course, I have kept the faith:

Henceforth there is laid up for me a crown of righteousness, which the Lord, the righteous judge, shall give me at that day: and not to me only, but unto all them that love his appearing."
11 Timothy 4:7-8

CORONATION SERVICE
of
KELLAND KEITH JEFFORDS, SR.
1928 - 1987

RAINBOW CHURCH OF GOD
4031 RAINBOW DRIVE
DECATUR, GEORGIA 30034

April 24, 1987

KELLAND KEITH JEFFORDS, SR.

Husband of

Nelia Flowers Jeffords

CHILDREN

Dianne Lawson Roswell, Georgia	4 children Michael, Eric & Derek, Mathew
Kelland Keith Jeffords, Jr. Decatur, Georgia	No Children
Danita Florance Plymouth, Minnesota	No Children

OTHER

Mrs. Isabel Jeffords Waresboro, Georgia	Mother
Raymond C.Jeffords Waresboro, Georgia	Brother
Mrs. Marilyn O'Steen Valdosta, Georgia	Sister

- CORONATION SERVICE -

- FRIDAY, APRIL 24,1987 - 2:00 P.M.

Service under the direction of
Rev. Paul F. Henson

Call to Worship   Rev. J. Edgar Waters

"To God Be The Glory"
Hymn No. 20

Scripture &Remarks   Rev. E.P. Pruett

"My Tribute"   Nelia Jeffords

THE MINISTERIAL YEARS

1951 – 1956   Rev. Clarence Busby

Special Song   Jeffords Children
                                                  Keith, Dianne & Danita

"Till The Storm Passes By"

1956 – 1966   Rev. Gerald Bailey

Congregational Hymn.   *"Blessed Assurance"* Hymn No. 133

.1966 – 1967   Rev. H.B. Ramsey

Special Song *"It Matters to Him"*   *Rick Copeland*

1967 – 1970   Rev. Steve Land

1970 – 1974   Rev. Merlin Brown

Prayer and Remarks   Dr. Lamar Vest
                                                  Asst. Gen. Overseer
                                                       Church of God

Special Song   *"I'll Never Pass This Way Again"* Jerry Rushing

1974 – 1980   Rev. Jim Bolin

Statistics and Remarks   Dr. Robert E. Fisher
                                             North Ga. State Overseer
                                                       Church of God

1980 – 1987   Rev. James Fain
                                                  Rev. Luther Nance
                                               Rev. David McBrayer

Congregational Hymn   *"Victory In Jesus"*
                                                     Hymn No. 182

Closing Remarks   Rev. Paul F. Henson

- INTERMENT SERVICE -

SATURDAY, APRIL 25,1987
2:00 P.M.

Pinecrest Memorial Gardens
Jesup, Georgia

Officiating Ministers:

Rev. J. Edgar Waters

Rev. Bruce Flowers

- SPECIAL THANKS -

You have shown your kindness by attendance today to share in the Coronation Service in honor of Kelland. We've been blessed with your love, prayers, and enduring friendships which we cherish.

To all of you, we say "Thank You" for memorable moments today.

Nelia,
Granny,
& children

MINISTERIAL CHRONOLOGY

Attended Bible Training School, Sevierville, TN

Lee College, Cleveland, TN

Oglethorpe University, Atlanta, GA

Ministerial License — 1951

Ordination - July 21, 1959

STATE YOUTH & CHRISTIAN EDUCATION
DIRECTOR 1970 - 1974

BOARDS SERVED:

State Council
State Evangelism Board
State Trustee
State Youth & Christian Education Board Ministerial Examination
Board

CHURCHES SERVED:

Associate Pastor Hemhill Ave. Church of God
  (Mt. Paran Church Church of God)

Organized & Pastor - E. Albany Church of God

Griffin - Palace Street Church of God (Central Lake)

Dayton, Ohio E. 4th Street Church of God

Atlanta - Southside Church of God

Mableton - Church of God

Rainbow - Decatur, Church of God

Chapter 12

Lee University Scholarship Endowed

Keith was instrumental in the endowment of the scholarship. His dad so loved by Georgians that the concept of a scholarship in his name was the right way to go. This would perpetuate his ministry while assisting Georgia students financially to achieve their educational goals. Keith received many scholarships while attending Emory University. He knew Lee College scholarships would do the same for Lee students.

A dinner was planned, guests were invited, and plans for the **Kelland Jeffords Scholarship** were endowed with thousands of dollars. Many thanks to my sister and brother-in-law, Rev. and Mrs. J. Edgar Waters, and my nephew, Robert Earl Waters, who hosted the dinner at River Bottom Restaurant, Jonesboro, GA.

The scholarship continues to give financial aid to Georgia students at Lee University.

In 1989, Danita and Bob became the proud parents to *Robert Glenn Florance IV*. This makes five grandsons. All handsome, loving, Christian young men that would make any grandparent thrilled.

The four Lawson grandsons are all graduates of Lee University and recipients of the *Kelland Jeffords Scholarship*. Glenn will graduate from high school in 2008.

Three generations of Kelland Jeffords family members are graduates of Lee University. I support our college financially. **The Kelland Jeffords Scholarship** for Georgia students is an open scholarship for all majors. The **Nelia F. Jeffords Scholarship** is for Music Majors in the Graduate School of Music open to all students.

At this writing I have five great-grandchildren. Eric and Jennifer are the parents of three: Ethan, Emily and Ryan.

Derek and Carlyn are the parents of two: Anthony, Aden and a daughter due in March 2007.

Michael, Matthew, and Glenn will make their contribution later in life when they are married.

Unfortunately, Kelland didn't live to see one of his grandsons, Glenn Florance, who was born in 1989. The great-grandchildren have since made their entry helping populate the Jeffords Family.

Back row: Derek, Eric, Glenn
Front row: Michael, Nelia, Matthew

Jen and Eric Lawson
Ryan. Emily, Ethan

Carlyn and Derek Lawson
Aden and Anthony

Chapter 13

Our Tribute

by Dianne, Keith, Danita
And Michael

Dianne Jeffords

Dianne Jeffords

Dianne Jeffords

<u>Awards and Honors</u>

- 5 time Platinum Record recipient
- 1st Place Winner, Piano Solo Division, International Teen Competition, St. Louis, MO
- 1st Place Winner, Directing & Arranging, International Teen Competition Kansas City, MO
- Georgia Country Music Award, Songwriting Competition, for the song written "State of Confusion"
- Jr. Miss Pageant Talent Award Recipient
- Unanimous Superior Plus ratings in various national piano auditions

Performance and Recording

- Tours in USA including Hawaii; London, Austria, Bavaria, Germany
- Radio and television: Channel 46, Channel 5, Channel 36 WAEC Love 86, TBN, Atlanta Alive
- Featured soloist and accompanist on two RCA label recordings
- Studio pianist for various Atlanta & Nashville recording studios
- Chattanooga Symphony Orchestra, Chattanooga, TN; Civic Auditorium, Richmond, VA; Kyle Auditorium, St. Louis, MO; Municipal Auditorium, Dayton, OH; National Hemisphere Pageant, Philadelphia, PA; Civic Auditorium, Dayton, OH; National Hemisphere Pageant, Philadelphia, PA; Civic Auditorium, Dallas, TX; Municipal Auditorium, Kansas City, MO
- In Atlanta: Atlantis Productions, Alliance Theatre, Axtel Productions, Emory University, Atlanta Civic Center; GA State University, Maynard Jackson, Mayor of Atlanta Inaugural Dinner; Jimmy Carter, President of the United States, Political Fundraiser; Dorsey School for the Performing Arts, Social Security Administration Annual Convention, Robert Shaw Institute, Emory University; Various hotels including Ritz Carlton, Hilton, Hyatt Regency, JW Marriott

Songwriting and A&R

- Song written "Nothing Is Impossible" recorded and published by Spirit Sound Music 1993
- Song written "His Angels" published by Joste Publishing; recording by Platinum Entertainment 1997
- A&R Coordinator for Platinum Entertainment Records

Dianne and Four Young Sons

Dianne and Four Grown Sons

Kelland Keith Jeffords, Jr., MD, DDS

TRIBUTE TO MY DAD

How does one write briefly about your father? I was fortunate to have my dad for 27 years. Much has been written about his ministry and the impact on his parishioners, community, and fellow ministers. My dad's ministry was effective and he achieved success early because of hard work. He also had my mom. Together, they were a team. Each strengthened the effectiveness of there collaborative efforts. Whether is was breaking the Church of God's national Sunday School attendance record or raising monies for Youth World Evangelism Appeal, mom was there contributing.

My dad was named after Clarence Budington Kelland, a popular early 20th century writer. My grandmother had read many of his short stories in the Saturday Evening Post and liked his name. My father lived up to the uniqueness of his name.

The son of storekeepers in the small Georgia town of Waresboro, he was raised in an environment of conversation. Like my grandparents, dad enjoyed talking. Waresboro was filled with many colorful neighbors. Many of them congregated at Jeffords' Grocery or on the circular sofa of my grandparents' living room. Granny Jeffords often said, "let's go into the living room and talk it out". Story telling was developed into an art form. This influenced my dad's congenial personality and affected his future ministry.

Living with dad was as unique as his name. He was equally colorful at home. If my friends called my house, they usually ended up with an extended conversation with my dad. A restless sleeper, we would often find him asleep in the den or other locations in the house. I remember coming home from Lee College one weekend. Sleeping in my room, I remember having someone sit on me. As I screamed and my dad nearly had a heart attack, we regrouped and he slept in the other twin bed in my room. He stated he forgot I was home. Mom used to say she made more beds each day than anyone.

Our home was always a boarding house with many college-aged folks staying to work with the church or reorient their lives. Mom always made extra food to feed the walk-ins that come at every family supper. The conversations around the dinner table were predictable: church stuff and our day. He loved talking about church growth. He used to say that there was always a reason why churched never grew…the church didn't want to grow.

Traveling with dad was always an experience. If he was driving, the traveling time was increased with stops at country stores to have a coke with the locals. Dad would always find someone that knew someone. He found that six degrees of separation from Kelland Jeffords. He loved waving at others in cars. He also drove very slowly. When people would pass him in anger, dad would also give them a wave and smile. He drove slowly because he was always talking.

During our return to Georgia from his pastorate in Ohio, he stopped the car and got into the median of I-75. He got on his hands and knees kissing the dirt and yelling, "O Georgia, I will never leave you again". We were embarrassed to death. Dad remained in Georgia for the rest of his professional life.

My dad had a passion for purchasing "bargain" cars. He had an old Volkswagon Beetle for years. During the brief stay in Ohio, the bottom of the car began to rust from the salty slush on the snowy roads. After moving to Georgia, the rear floorboards gave way piece by piece. Dad only got rid of this car after a near financial disaster. Mom and Ruth Pace (wife of Reverend Ray Pace that preceded dad as Youth and Christian Education Director of Georgia) had gone for some ice cream during Youth Camp season. Ruth had the youth camp tuition money for deposit in a bag. While going into Baskin Robbins for ice cream, Ruth placed the money bag under her passenger seat. When they returned to the Campground, the money was gone. Ruth's deposit bag had fallen out of the hole in the floorboard. Retracing their trip, the money was found in the parking lot where they had parked (and the money had fallen out of the car).

After this incident, dad replaced the Volkswagon with a Ford Falcon. He purchased this car from an elderly lady that rarely drove the car. Another bargain. This car was not fashionable. Rather homely. My dad drove this car with pride. Already old, this car was used daily for visitation and other ministerial duties. The wear and tear began to take its toll. The front passenger door would not stay closed. If you went around a corner, the door would fly open. Reverend Jim Bolin tells a story of riding in this Falcon. While turning a corner, Jim leaned against the door and ultimately falling out a moving vehicle. Thankfully, dad was driving slowly and Jim was not hurt.

As I have reflected on my childhood, I remembered what sacrifices my parents made for the successes of their children. Trumpets were purchased and I was given private lessons with Atlanta Symphony professionals. Dad would drive me to lessons and wait in the car. I would often find him asleep in a hot or cold car. Both parents were always present at school events and concerts. As kids, we were included in the work of the church. As we became teenagers, their interests in youth ministry heightened. Our life always returned to the church. So did our musical skills.

The ultimate story of love I think happened while I was at Lee College. My Volkswagon Beetle became stuck in first gear. Dad drove to Cleveland and gave me a spare car. Then he drove back to Mableton in first gear. At a max speed of 10-15 miles per hour, it took him a whole day. He never complained and said he enjoyed the trip, stopping several times to converse with locals. I can't imagine another father doing this.

A unique event in my life was the day we all met my future brother-in-law, Bob Florance. He was coming over to our home to pick up Danita for a date. Danita had inform us that Bob was raised Catholic. Our family just happened to have company in our home, Lamar and Ardys McDaniel. Dad told Lamar that they should see if this young man would be deserving of Danita. When Bob arrived, he was escorted into the living room where Dad and Lamar would share the "Gospel" with him. He was double teamed on a variety of subjects from dating etiquette to the sinner's prayer. Years later, Bob recanted that he was probably the only man in America that met both his future father-in-law and step father-in-law at the same time.

My last conversation with my dad was regarding my career. So typical. During the last few days of his conscious life, I was deeply involved with Emory University School of Dentistry's "Clinic Day". I was coordinating this two-day event and had just picked up our keynote speaker from the airport. He was quite interested to know about this speaker, Dr. James Edwards, former South Carolina Governor and Reagan's Secretary of Energy. Dr. Edwards was also an Oral and Maxillofacial Surgeon that was the President of Medical University of South Carolina. Dad wanted to know all of the details. I had also been accepted for Oral and Maxillofacial Surgery externships at several universities. He helped me decide on which university to accept.

These are the final moments of conversation with my dad. It was so appropriate because he was supportive of my endeavors throughout my life. Even his last known conversation was regarding his family. Clarence Busby visited my father just before he lapsed into unconsciousness. Dad asked Clarence to represent him at my dental school graduation. He had a premonition that he would not survive his strokes. He was right.

Clarence did attend my graduation and sat with my mother. A happy day was filled with reflection of my father. Subsequent momentous occasions still have moments of sadness with the remembrance of dad's absence.

When my father was near death, I told my mother that she would have my permission to remarry. I wanted her to know that her life was not going to die with my dad. Seven years later, mom remarried another preacher from Waresboro, Georgia. Lamar McDaniel was a life-long friend of my father. His first wife, Ardys, was also a friend and had died after a long and painful struggle with breast cancer. He has provided mother with companionship, love, and a continuation of ministry. He has been a good father to me. My stepfather also cherishes the memories of Kelland Jeffords, making the circle complete.

K. Keith Jeffords, Jr.MD,DDS

Keith Jeffords

Keith's Graduation From Emory University

Graduation at Emory University
President Lamey awards Keith
"Marion Luther Britton Award"

Keith with Dr. Lois Beach
Easter Virginia Medical School Graduation

CURRICULUM VITAE

K. KEITH JEFFORDS, JR.

ADDRESSES

Home: 1275 West Spring Street   *Office:* 3964 Atlanta Road
      Smyrna, Georgia   30080   Smyrna, Georgia   30080

EDUCATION

Eastern Virginia Medical School   Doctor of Medicine
Norfolk, Virginia   July 1995

Emory University   Doctor of Dental Surgery
Atlanta, Georgia   May 1988

Lee University   Bachelor of Science
Cleveland, Tennessee   (Honors) May 1981

South Cobb High School   Diploma
Austell, Georgia   (Highest Honors) June 1977

POSTDOCTORAL TRAINING

University of Pittsburgh   Plastic Surgery Residency
Pittsburgh, Pennsylvania   July 1998- June 2000

Pennsylvania State University   Plastic Surgery
Hershey, Pennsylvania   July 1997- June 1998

Eastern Virginia Medical School   General Surgery
Norfolk General Hospital   Residency
Norfolk, Virginia   July 1995- June 1997

University of Miami   Oral and Maxillofacial Surgery
Jackson Memorial Hospital   Residency

Miami, Florida   July 1989- June 1993

Harvard University   General Practice Residency
Brigham and Women's Hospital   July 1988- June 1989
Boston, Massachusetts

ACADEMIC APPOINTMENTS

South University   Clinical Faculty
Physician Assistant Program   2005 - present
Savannah, Georgia

University of Pittsburgh   Clinical Fellow
School of Medicine   July 1998- June 2000
Pittsburgh, Pennsylvania

Harvard University   Clinical Fellow
School of Dental Medicine   July 1988- 1989
Boston, Massachusetts

LICENSURE AND CERTIFICATION

American Board of Plastic Surgery- **Board Certified, 2002**
Georgia- Board of Medicine- #049041
Georgia- Board of Dentistry- #10634
Pennsylvania- Board of Medicine- #MD- 062343-L (inactive)
Virginia- Board of Medicine- #0101-054383 (inactive)
Northeast Regional Board of Dental Examiners- May 1988

PRESENT ACTIVITIES

American Society of Plastic Surgeons, active member
National Alumni Board, Eastern Virginia Medical School, Norfolk,
Virginia, 2000-present
National Academy of Recording Arts and Sciences, member
Atlanta Symphony Orchestra Chorus: 2000 to present; 1981-85
Talent Development Program Advisory Board, Atlanta Symphony
Orchestra, 2000-2004

RESEARCH EXPERIENCE

1987 NIDR Summer Fellowship: "Separation and Characterization of Osteoclast Lipids"

1986 NIDR Summer Fellowship: "Effects of 1,25-Dihydroxyvitamin D3 Induced Phosphoinositides

1979 NSF Grant, Lee University: "Butylated Hydroxytoluene: Effects on Cardiotoxicity of Adriamycin in Laboratory Mice"

PUBLICATIONS

MacKay D, Mazahari M, Graham WP, Jeffords K, Leber D, Gorman P, Lieser JD, Wrye S, Kutz R, Saggers G. "Incidence of Operative Procedures on Cleft Lip and Palate Patients" Annals of Plastic Surgery, 1999, 42:445-8.

Blackburn JH, Boemi L, Hall WW, Jeffords KK, Hauck RM, Banducci DR, Graham WP. "Negative Pressure Dressings as a Bolster for Skin Grafts", Annals of Plastic Surgery, 1998; 40:453-7.

1998 Coding Illustrated: Head and Neck. Keith Jeffords, Technical Editor. Salt Lake City: Medicode Publications, January 1998, pp 1-795.

Heit, Stevens, and Jeffords. "Comparison of Ceftriaxone with Penicillin for Antibiotic Prophylaxis for Compound Mandible Fractures", Oral Surgery, Oral Medicine, and Oral Pathology, April 1997, pp 423-6.

Coders' Desk Reference. Keith Jeffords, Technical Contributor. Salt Lake City: Medicode Publications, August 1995, pp 1-725.

Coding Illustrated- Midface: Skeletal Structures of the Nose and Orbit. Keith Jeffords, Technical Editor. Salt Lake City: Medicode Publications, May 1994, pp 1-167.

Coding Illustrated- Midface: Maxillary Soft Tissue. Keith Jeffords, Technical Editor. Salt Lake City: Medicode Publications, March 1994, pp 1-223.

Coding Illustrated- Midface: Maxillary Bone and Dentition. Keith Jeffords, Technical Editor. Salt Lake City: Medicode Publications, February 1994, pp 1-152.

Coding Illustrated- Midface: Sinus and Nasal Mucosa. Keith Jeffords, Technical Editor. Salt Lake City: Medicode Publications, December 1994, pp 1-200.

PRESENTATIONS

2005 American Society of Aesthetic Plastic Surgeons, New Orleans, Louisiana, "Radiesse for Lipoatrophy in the HIV-positive Patient", May 2005 (Neavin, Jeffords, Manders).

2004 University of Alabama Plastic Surgery Ground Rounds, "Gynecomastia", June 2004

2000 American Society of Plastic Surgeons, Los Angeles, California, "Clinical Uses for Gamma Graft", October 2000

1998 Northeastern Society of Plastic Surgeons, Newport, Rhode Island, "Incidence of Operative Procedures for the Treatment of Cleft Disorders, October 1998

1998 Robert Ivy Society of Plastic Surgeons, Hershey, Pennsylvania, "Complications Resulting from the Treatment of Wounds with Negative Pressure", March 1998

1993 University of Miami Alumni Meeting, Aventura, Florida, "Free Fat Grafts: Indications and Review of Harvesting Techniques", June 1993

1993 Lee University Science Alumni Association," Current Therapy in Orthognathic Surgery", September 1993

1992 University of Miami Alumni Meeting, Key Biscayne, Florida, "Current Concepts in Treatment of Naso-Orbital-Ethmoidal Fractures", June 1992

1988 Hinman Dental Society of Georgia, winter meeting, Atlanta, Georgia, January 1988

1987 American Dental Association Annual Session/ Dentsply Student Clinician Program, Las Vegas, Nevada, October 1987

RELEVANT WORK EXPERIENCE

Center for Wound Care Emory- Adventist Hospital Smyrna, Georgia	Medical Director August 2001- July 2002
Aesthetic Plastic and Reconstructive Surgeons-Private Practice Atlanta, Georgia	July 2000- 2002
Oral and Maxillofacial Surgery Pocomoke City, Maryland	Part-time Private Practice November 1993- June 1995
Medicode Publications Salt Lake City, Utah	Technical Editor/ Consultant 1994- 1999
Hyperbaric Medicine UM/ Jackson Memorial Hospital Miami, Florida	Medical Observer/ Operator 1992-93, part-time
Smith Kline Bioscience Labs Atlanta, Georgia	Staff Toxicologist 1981-86, full and part-time

HONORS AND AWARDS

The Stephen H. Miller Award, 1998- for outstanding teaching by a Plastic Surgery Resident. The Pennsylvania State University College of Medicine

Upsilon Xi Alumnus of the Year, 1995, Lee University

The Marion Luther Brittain Award, 1988, Emory University- the
highest University-wide award given annually to only one Emory
student at the general University commencement ceremony which is
intended as "a public and permanent expression of gratitude for
service to the University rendered without expectation of reward or
recognition".

American Association of Orthodontists Award, 1988

Dean's Leadership Award, 1988

Who's Who Among Students in American Colleges and Universities,
1988

Emory University- ADA/Dentsply Student Clinician competition,
1987, 1st place

American Student Dental Association- Region V "Delegate of the
Year", 1986

Ty Cobb Foundation Scholarship: 1985-88
Emile T. Fisher Scholarship: 1986
Emory University Merit Tuition Scholarship: 1986-88
Perrin Scholarship: 1985-86
Trebor Scholarship: 1984-85
Joseph Whitehead Scholarship: 1986-88

Lee University- Distinguished Science Alumnus, 1984

Danita Kay Jeffords Florance

A WALK WITH MY DAD

Take the "Lawrence Welk" show, transform it into a Christian variety hour, and it would closely mirror the daily routine of my life as a member of the Jeffords household. Being the youngest of three, you can only imagine that my perspective of life at home was slightly different than my older siblings. I was for quite some time the spare, and in my younger years, I was often times shy and pretty much along for the ride. My reflection of our home was a house that never stood still. There were certain things that you could always count on such as music playing in just about every room, the aroma of my mothers wonderful southern food, visitors roaming throughout the house, and planning sessions that would last until dawn. As a young child, I cannot recall there being an exact bedtime. You slept when you could and wherever you could. Often times this meant a bench at the church with hymnals as your pillow, a spare couch because your room would have a guest in it, or sharing a bed with a sibling who was not always happy to give up their extra space. Growing up a "Jeffords", there was a natural assumption that your birthright was that of a musician. Well it was true! Yes, every one of us was born with a desire to perform. In my younger years, wherever my dad spoke, we would sing. I am not referring to one or two songs, but a mini concert. All of us would perform various musical acts, but my fondest memories were when my father and mother would sing their favorite songs, which were "Till the Storm Passes Over" and "Never Turn Back". Oh how these powerful songs were such a blessing to people. Even though we were not aware, every time my parents sang they demonstrated to their children how music was such a vital portion of ministry. We were certainly multi-talented and outstanding musicians in our respective talents. We sang, played various instruments, composed, and even directed. We never complained as we realized that God had given us all a special gift. We were a team and gleaned from our parents the passion of music.

My Dad was so proud of each of us. Often times he would make tremendous sacrifices so that we could have the best musical teachers. For me, that included voice lessons, piano, acting and dancing. Around ninth grade, I became very involved in musical theatre, commercial film, and motion pictures. Never did my parents discourage me, even though this was a controversial subject within religious circles. When I landed leading roles in musicals and film, my parents collectively supported my craft, handled the criticism of skeptics with a strong resolve, and thwarted off the negatives by implementing the positives. For the most part, my dad was usually the one that took me to my lessons because my mother had a part time job. Never complaining, he would drive great distances and wait very patiently until I was finished. My dad was a man of love, always seeing the positive side of everyone and every situation. For example, when I would come out of my classes, my dad always had his window down so he could enjoy the sounds around him. He would soak up and watch all of the nature around, explaining how what he had seen related to human life. Dad was an animated storyteller and whenever he had the opportunity, he inadvertently, through the simplicities of everyday life, would give you a Godly life lesson. This was one of his unique ways of showing you how much he cared.

My father loved to talk with you one-on-one. He would always choose the car as his favorite place to converse because he had your full attention, and you could not escape! As far as parenting goes, my parents had it easy, as my siblings and I were obliging kids. But as I came into my teen years, and even though my parents had been through the travails of raising my older sister, they were not through parenting yet! You see, when you have girls, you also have admirers. And boy oh boy did we ever. However, like any other obstacle thrown in my dad's way, he handled it with a sense of humor and calm timing. My dad found it quite amusing at the volume of admirers that would show up unannounced. Dad would always invite then in, chat with them for a while, and eventually see them to the door with a "Be good and have a nice day". This was his way of weeding out the worthy and unworthy. Often times I was clueless that I even had a visitor. It would be hours or even days until my dad would say in passing, "Oh by the way, I had a nice conversation with....". He was such a good sport that he helped a suitor pull their car up a steep hill covered in ice, was the front man for me when several unannounced admirers showed up at the same time, and even took a few to the bus station. As always, my dad never missed a step when it came to the make-up and character of others. He was quick with discernment and wise with advice. So, whenever my dad could seize any car time with me, he took full advantage of it. These trips were some of my fondest memories of our time spent together. It was a place that I had my dad all to myself. He would always ask me a series of questions with Godly advice to follow. Even though I would cringe at times of embarrassment, I knew that my dad had my best interest at heart, as I am certain these talks saved me from making mistakes more than I realized. I am told that my dad got a kick out of my numerous friends and all the drama it added to our household. He never made a big fuss or forbid me with heavy chastisement, but always treated me with love, understanding and compassion. Life in the car with my dad was always adventurous, and some of the best trips of my life.

My Father's passing was especially hard on me as I was only 23 years of age and just going into my third year of marriage. I can remember as if it were yesterday the phone call of my mother saying that my father was in the hospital. Those days were some of the darkest and most challenging days of my life, because they were to be my last days spent with him. The pain that one feels is all encompassing when a loved one is nearing death. Each day at the hospital was agonizing for my family and me as they were filled with touch-and-go, life-threatening moments. But, in the midst of the darkness, it felt as if a bright light glowed in my father's room. Each family member took turns by my father's bedside. We read scripture, played music, sang songs, and prayed for a miracle. It was during this time that my walk with Christ and the foundation of my faith became stronger. Each day was a day of walking in faith, as faith was our only hope. I also came to realize that even though people all around the world were praying for us, it was our walk with the Lord that was going to bring the comfort we needed. Each day that we kept a vigil around my dad's bed was filled with quiet and still moments, and a day of great spiritual growth. In spite of the circumstances, God poured out his spirit on each of us. The last hours of my dad's life were filled with music. My mother, brother, mother's sister Aletha, her husband Edgar and I encamped around my father's bed. As we stood joining hands all around him, we began to sing some of my dad's favorite songs and choruses. As we sang in family harmony, the Holy Spirit filled the room and there was a calming presence that came upon us all. The nurses that had been attending to my dad for several weeks also joined us in song and prayer. We sang for a couple of hours and at the end of our songs, my uncle led us in a joyful prayer. That was to be the first night in weeks that my father lay completely still. Each one of us felt God's presence and there was no doubt that angels surrounded my father. The tranquility that fell upon the room was a peace like I had never experienced. It was just two hours later that my father was taken home to be with the Lord.

The absence of my father has been a devastation to all that knew him. He was a unique man who possessed wisdom, discernment, and a love of people that could only be given from God. There is not a day that my father is not in my thoughts. There is not a family gathering that his presence is not felt and his name is not mentioned. His legacy lives on in each of us who were his family and friends. My siblings and I have many of his traits, and for this we are so blessed. Even my son who never knew him has come to know him through the countless stories told by his cousins. He even possesses a compassionate spirit and sensitivity that is a great likeness to my father. As a grown woman, I can now appreciate all of the teachings of my father, and realize more than ever his greatness as a man. For this I am most grateful for my Godly heritage. Goodnight my father as you are greatly loved and missed. Until we meet again.

Danita Florance

Danita Florance

Glenn, Danita and Bob in Hawaii

Danita Florance's Bio

Danita Florance is the Director/Owner of Premiere School of Self-Improvement and Professional Modeling in Duluth, Georgia. She has a Bachelor of Science degree in Retail Merchandising from the University of Minnesota. She is both a professional model and actress, and has been featured in national television, motion pictures and print advertisements for companies such as McDonalds, Dr. Pepper, Coca-Cola, Tultex Corporation, Leone's Films, and Tri-Star Pictures.

As a renowned pageant specialist, Danita has personally coached numerous queen contest winners throughout the United States on the local, state, and national levels for such systems including: Teen of America, National Teenager, Teen USA, Miss America, Miss USA, Mrs. America, Mrs. United States and many more.

Danita holds teaching certificates for modeling in Georgia/Minnesota, as well as certifications from the Weist Barron School of Television and Sandra Dorsey School of Performing Arts. She has taught modeling in the Cobb and Gwinnett County Community Schools. As a Choreographer, Danita has produced numerous couture fashion shows for various establishments and schools in Georgia and Minnesota.

As a native Atlantan, Danita holds the title of Miss National Harvest Queen, Teen All American, Mrs. Georgia Beauties of America 1999, Mrs. Georgia Globe 2000, Mrs. Georgia United States 2001 and a Top Ten National Finalist at the Mrs. United States Pageant which was televised on the Fox network. She was also a top five finalist in the Miss Georgia USA, Dogwood Festival, and North Georgia Fair systems.

Danita is an accomplished musician in vocal performance and has been a member of the broadway touring company "Atlantis Productions", DeKalb Players, Screen Actors Guild and has held leading roles performing in numerous plays, broadway musicals, and for Government dignitaries throughout the United States and Europe.

Danita is known best for her ability to transform undiscovered talent into a polished performer thereby helping them to fulfill their life long dreams. She is very proud to be nominated by the Gwinnett Chamber of Commerce Governors board for the- 2004 "Outstanding Leadership Program."

Danita Jeffords-Florance, Mrs. Georgia 2001

Robert Glenn Florance, IV

Michael Lawson

My Granddad: A Lesson in Life

I was young when my grandfather passed. I had just turned thirteen, in fact. At that age, it is difficult to qualify what death means... even when someone close to you leaves. Yet, I knew then that I had lost a person that had made an impression that wouldn't fade. The true testament to Granddad's ministry and life is that there are so many that feel this exact way. His story is littered with people that he loved, and who loved him in return. This small piece of writing is an attempt to express how I felt, and still feel for him.

By all accounts, Granddad was a jokester. When I say this, I don't mean practical jokes, necessarily, but one who always had a funny story to tell. I've yet to meet someone who knew him that doesn't have a story involving Granddad, or some story that they heard him tell, and have subsequently co-opted. He was that guy. He made people laugh. It was one of his definitive characteristics. I still laugh at some of the crazy stories he would tell my brothers and me about his childhood friends. Don't get me wrong, he was as intelligent and perspicacious as any, but he refused to let these qualities strictly define him. But that only tells part of the story. You see, by the time I grew to know Granddaddy... really know him... he was very sick. He had been fighting acute Diabetes for a while, and this disease had taken its toll. He was, in many ways, a shell of the man that he used to be. Through this, though, he taught me lessons that I am still learning today.

Granddaddy once told me, "Son, people are going to disappoint you, but that doesn't give you a right to disappoint them.". I know... it's kind of corny. Yet, it's true. He said it to me more than once... and he was right. One of the things that I learned from my time with him is that family and friends are central to happiness. Due to family circumstances, I spent a great deal of time with my grandparents as a child. One of the things that always baffled me during my visits was the attention that he received. In my youthful mind, it was hard for me to understand why so many people would come and visit for hours. Whether in person or on the telephone, Granddad always had someone to speak with. It wasn't until much later that I realized that he had spent so much of his life investing in others, that they were now investing in him. I was never a witness to his full- time ministry, but I was privy to something as extraordinary, I think; the love that he had given was given back to him in his time of need. There's a lesson in that... one that I still have to learn on a daily basis.

In life, things happen that are, shall we say, unexpected. But we are expected to deal with them, nonetheless. My youngest brother, Matthew, at the age of, maybe, 1 year old, if that, fell and cracked his forehead on a stone fireplace, one benign evening at the Jeffords' house, and it was traumatic. Everyone in the house was scared... it was sudden... and it was dangerous. As I recall, my mom and grandmother shuttled Matthew to the ER and had him stitched up. Again, as I remember it, Granddad wanted to go the hospital, but couldn't. He couldn't drive a car due to the illness, and he had three very young grandchildren still in his home. I tell this story only because it exemplifies his life. Granddaddy pulled me aside and said, "We need to pray for your brother, Matthew. Go get your brothers". And we prayed. Truth be told, I didn't pay much attention to the prayer, because I was scared. The point is that he probably knew that three little boys, under the age of 8, wouldn't earnestly pray, but he did it anyway. He believed it, and he knew that there was a lesson there. He gave us the only thing he had at that moment...his faith.

True faith in Christ is something that we all aspire to. I learned a great deal about faith and fortitude from my grandfather. One of the lasting memories I have of him was listening to a college football game in his living room. He was an avid University of Georgia fan, and one autumn afternoon, I remember listening to Larry Munson call a game against the University of Clemson on the radio. It had been a tight game. It was close, and UGA had a field goal opportunity to win it... but it was from 59 yards or so (not an ideal situation when one is trying to win). Kevin Butler, the place kicker for Georgia, made it with two seconds left in the game... effectively, winning the ballgame. I had not seen my Granddad that animated in a long time, if ever. This moment made me a UGA fan forever, but more importantly, it was an opening for him to teach me one of the many life lessons that I carry with me today. After a few minutes, maybe hours, I was talking to him about the game, and he used that opportunity to teach me about the idea of perseverance and the importance of not quitting in life. What I couldn't understand then is that he might have been talking about his situation. He knew he was sick, but I never heard him complain. It would have been easy, and certainly understandable, for him to grow bitter and angry about his physical deterioration in his last few years, but he didn't. This man who had been so actively jovial and gregarious his entire life, was now a shadow of his former physical self. Yet, he showed nothing but grace and humor until the end. This, no doubt, was attributable to his relationship with his savior. You see, he held a faith in Christ that was stronger than his physical weakness. This, of course, was lost on me as a child. Now, as an adult, I look back and realize the gift he gave us in his example of faith in action. If I, during my life, can show a third of this kind of humility and devotion to my family, and those around me, I will have accomplished something, in deed.

There are so many things that I could write about: The times where we (my brothers and I) were 'rough housing', and he would call out for us to 'stop killing each other'... the times where he would pay 'the first one of us' to find his glasses or the hidden candy that was dispersed throughout the kitchen. There are so many things to say about so many wonderful memories, and I speak for my brothers, Eric, Derek, and Matthew, and my cousin Glenn, when I say that he still informs who we are as people today. Kelland Jeffords was a sweet and gentle man who loved the Lord. He was intensely and fiercely loyal to his family and friends, and repaid the loyalty given him with a kind of spirit and love that one finds only a few times in his or her life. When staying with him, and on a regular basis, granddad would call the grandkids in, one by one, and sit us down, and ask, "So, what do you want to do you with your life…. if you could do anything...?" As children we would always say the things that children usually say… a baseball player, a doctor, a lawyer... but, really, we had no clue. The thing is… I can answer that question now. I want to be more like him.

W. Michael Lawson Jr.

W. Michael Lawson Jr.

3012 Monument Avenue, #7
Richmond, Virginia 23221

Educational History
- Candidate for Master's of Arts Degree, University of Richmond, Richmond, Virginia, May 2007.
- Bachelor of Arts Degree, Magna Cum Laude, Lee University, Cleveland, Tennessee, July 2000.
- High school diploma, Byne Memorial High School, Albany, Georgia, 1992.

Professional History
- June 2005 to present, Personal Banker, Bank of America.

- 2004-2005, Full Graduate Assistant for Research and Teaching purposes, University of Richmond.

- 2003-2004, Graduate Assistant for Research, Dr. Ricardo Salvatore, University of Richmond.

- 2000-2003, Independent Contractor and Sales Manager, Cellular Sales Inc.

- 1998-1999, English Instructor for the BBC Foreign Language School, Jilin City, People's Republic of China.

Languages
- Spanish (functional)
- Chinese (Limited)

Awards and Commendations

- Full Research Fellow, University of Richmond, 2004-2005.
- Research Fellow, University of Richmond, 2003-2004.
- Excellence in Sales award, May 2003.
- Excellence in Sales award, April 2001.
- National Dean's List, 1997-1998,1999-2000.
- Who's Who for College Students, 2000.
- Departmental Award for Excellence in History, 1999-2000.
- Teaching Fellow, English Language Institute of China, 1998-1999.
- Research Fellow, Cambridge University, Cambridge, England, 1998.
- Teaching Assistant for Dr. Daniel Hoffman, Lee University, 1997-98, 1999-2000.

Dianne, Keith, Nelia and Dianne

Dianne, Bob and Danita, Nelia

Keith, Dianne, Nelia and Danita
Lee University Graduation

Keith in Berlin, Germany
Atlanta Symphony Chorus Tour

Chapter 14

POST: 4-22-1987

As I look back over the years and think from whence I came and what the Lord has enabled me to experience, I come one conclusion: *I am blessed!* The years spent with Kelland Jeffords in ministry enriched my life beyond measure.

Kelland and I grew in *faith* as we ministered the word to thousands during his thirty-seven years in ministry. Our *family*, the immediate and extended, have given us love and abundant blessings. The *friends* that we had before, and the ones we have come to know through the years, have buoyed us on to heights we could never have imagined. For this I am grateful!

I think of the opportunities that were given us and seized on to every one possible. Neither of us came from a minister's family, but rather from humble beginnings: parents who lived for God and loved the church. At an early age of six, I gave my heart to Christ. Kelland came to know Him personally in his teens.

In John 15: 16 "ye have not chosen me but I have chosen you, and ordained you, that ye should go and bring forth fruit, and that your fruit should remain:"

I am so glad the Lord *chose* Kelland and Nelia Jeffords to work in His kingdom. Whether we were teaching in a Sunday School Convention in Detroit, Michigan or Richmond, Virginia, an Evangelism Conference in San Juan, Puerto Rico or Mexico City, Mexico, we gladly served.

Maybe it was an associated youth trip to the Holy Land, part of the General Youth Department sponsored group to Germany for Y.W.E.A., an Evangelistic Outreach in Hawaii, or on a Missions trip to the Bahamas. Whenever possible we were reaching, teaching, and spreading the clarion call.

Nelia Jeffords

What a rich heritage! What great memories! What a wonderful life!
I am thankful that God chose us as part of His army to advance His
Kingdom. I am appreciative for – **"A Man Named Kelland."**

The World's Bible

Christ has no hands but our hands
To do His work today;
He has no feet but our feet
To lead men in His way.
He has no tongue but our tongues
To tell men how He died;
He has no help but our help
To bring them to His side.
We are the only Bible
The careless world will read.
We are the sinner's Gospel;
We are the scoffer's creed.
We are the Lord's last message
Given in deed and word
What if the type is crooked?
What if the print is blurred?
What if our hands are busy
With other work than His?
What if our feet are walking
Where sin's allurement is?
What if our tongues are speaking
Of things His lips would spurn?
How can we hope to help Him
And hasten His return?
To hasten our Lord's return,
We truly need much power;
So let us all be Spirit-filled,
And awaiting Him each hour.
In an hour that we think not,
He said He would appear;
Then let us walk in Holiness
And meet Him with a cheer.

-By A.J.F. and A.O.S.

ACKNOWLEDGMENTS

Paul L. Walker, Ph.D. Executive Bishop, Church of God Cleveland TN, Senior Pastor Emeritus Mount Paran Church of God, Atlanta, GA..

Steven J. Land, Ph.D. President/Professor Church of God Theological Seminary, Cleveland, TN.

Jim Bolin, B.S., Masters, Ordained Bishop, Senior Pastor Trinity Chapel Church of God, Powder Springs, GA.

Marcus D. Lamb, B.S. President/CEO - Daystar Television Network - Dallas, TX

Rodney Jeffords, Administrative Bishop, Church of God in Pennsylvania

Paul H. Henson, Retired. Formerly served as State Overseer, General Youth and Christian Education Director, Spirit Care Director, General Council of Eighteen.

Robert P. Herrin, B.S. Ordained Bishop, Senior Pastor Plant City Church of God, Plant City, FL.

Clayton Brown, Ordained Bishop, Senior Pastor Cedar Valley Church of God, Dalton, GA.

Ray Dawson, Ordained Bishop, Senior Pastor Union Grove Church of God, Tifton, GA.

J. Edgar Waters, Ordained Bishop Retired,. Former Pastor East Point Church of God, East Point, GA.

Lewis Stover, Ordained Bishop Retired,. Formerly served as Pastor, State Council, various boards in Georgia.

E. P. Pruett, Retired. Formerly served as General Presbyter Assemblies of God, State Superintendent and pastor.

E. Lamar McDaniel, Ph.D. Ordained Bishop, Pastor Emeritus Evangel Cathedral Church of God, Baltimore, MD., International Missionary Evangelist, presently serving as State Coordinator for Covenant Pastoral Leadership Development Initiative in Delmarva, DC., Cluster Elder.

Terrell McBrayer, Ed.D. Ordained Bishop Retired,. Formerly served as Pastor, Educator.

David L. Gibson, D.Min. Commander, U.S. Navy Chaplin Corps

Bob Johnson, Ph.D. Professor of Educational Leadership and Policy, University of Utah, Ordained Minister Church of God.
Tim Trotter, B.S. Lee University. Evangelist and noted lecturer.

Clarence Busby Jr., Ordained Bishop, Church of God and, forever a friend

Wm. Michael Lawson Jr. B.A. Lee University, Candidate for Master's of Arts Degree, University of Richmond, Richmond, Virginia, May 2007

Kelland Keith Jeffords, Jr. Doctor of Medicine, Eastern Virginia Medical School, Norfolk, Virginia. Doctor of Dental Surgery, Emory University, Atlanta, Georgia. Plastic Surgery Residency, Pittsburg, Pennsylvania. Oral and Maxillofacial Surgery Residency, University of Miami, Jackson Memorial General Hospital, Miami, Florida. General Practice Residency, Harvard University, Brigham and Women's Hospital, Boston, Massachusetts.

Jackie T. Walker, State Director of Women's Ministries, North Georgia Church of God State Office.

Darlia Conn, B.S. Lee University Teacher and Lecturer.

Danita Jeffords-Florance, B.S. University of Minnesota, Director/Owner of Premier School of Self-Improvement and Professional Modeling, Duluth, Ga. Currently holds the title of Mrs. Georgia. Also, nominated by Gwinnett Chamber of Commerce Governors Board for the 2004- "Outstanding Leadership Program."

Marilyn Jeffords-O'Steen, attended Lee College. Resides in Valdosta, Georgia.

Aletha Flowers-Waters, retired. Presently lives in Jesup, Georgia.

Dianne Jeffords, attended Lee University-accompanist Lee Singers. EMI Music Capitol Records Artist Development. Award winning pianist International Teen Talent-St. Louis, MO., she is known for her performance, songwriting and arranging expertise hi music.

I have included a CD of B. E. Underwood's sermon "Reach Out in Love". This was a favorite of both Kelland and me. It was recorded at a State Sunday School Conference held at the Mt. Paran Church of God in Atlanta, Georgia. Kelland planned this conference while he was Georgia's State Youth and Christian Education Director.

This sermon touched the lives of so many. Kelland and I often talked about the sermon and its impact on the ministers in the State of Georgia. It seemed to represent Kelland's ministry and the direction of his term as Youth and Christian Education Director. You will feel the intensity of this sermon as Dr. Underwood passionately delivers to the body of ministers on that Friday morning in 1973. To the hundreds in attendance this sermon opened a new dimension of ministry.

Kelland introduces the speaker, B. E. Underwood, and Clarence Busby, Sr. prays the closing prayer with comments. All three have gone to their eternal reward. The keepsake CD will be a cherished memento of these outstanding ministers. As you listen to the sermon, may your hearts be renewed afresh by the Holy Spirit and challenged to share the love of God to a world that is in need of Christ's love.

— Nelia